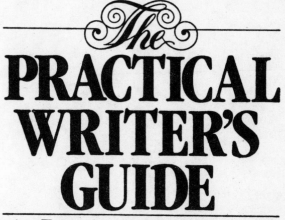

PRACTICAL WRITER'S GUIDE

An Easy-Access Source Book

Mary A. De Vries

WINGS BOOKS
NEW YORK • AVENEL, NEW JERSEY

This 1992 edition is published by Wings Books,
distributed by Outlet Book Company, Inc.,
a Random House Company,
40 Engelhard Avenue, Avenel, New Jersey 07001,
by arrangement with SIGNET/NAL Penguin Inc.

Printed and bound in the United States of America

Library of Congress Cataloging-in-Publication Data

De Vries, Mary Ann.
        The practical writer's guide : an easy-access source book / Mary
A. De Vries.
            p.   cm.
        Originally published: New York, N.Y. : New American Library,
c1986.
        Includes index.
        ISBN 0-517-08471-6 : $6.99
            1. English language—Rhetoric—Handbooks, manuals, etc.
2. English language—Grammar—1950—Handbooks, manuals, etc.
I. Title.
[PE1408.D378   1992]
808'.042—dc20
                                                                    92-18861
                                                                    CIP

To Robert J. De Vries

CONTENTS

Contents

PREFACE

Have you heard about the restaurant advertisement that said: WANTED—MAN TO WASH DISHES AND TWO WAITRESSES? I wonder how the waitresses felt about that. Another favorite of mine is the story about the man who noticed two potted plants strolling through the lobby of an office building. One immediately wonders what he drank for lunch. Stated properly, neither example would be as entertaining, but both could be easily corrected by moving or changing a few words. The restaurant notice might say: WANTED: TWO WAITRESSES AND DISHWASHER. The story might be changed to say that a man, strolling through the lobby of an office building, noticed two potted plants. Everyday life is full of such examples, and we all need to devote more attention to the way we put things in writing. But how can we improve our writing? How can we judge the accuracy and clarity of what we say?

Ever since Bo Derek gave new meaning to the number ten, writers have joined the craze to rate their work on a scale of one to ten. Not all writers and critics use this measure with tongue in cheek, either; numerical-rating devices are common academically and professionally. But you can view writing in many ways. Business writers often think in terms of effective or ineffective writing, and sales writers frequently classify writing as productive or unproductive. Such evaluations are used to tell you whether your writing is helping you to perform better at work and, in turn, to earn more money. Your interest in writing may be less financially or professionally motivated, though. You may think of writing strictly as an art or as a cultural activity. If you're primarily concerned with levels of *quality* in writing, columnist James Kilpatrick has just the measure for you. He said in his book *The Writer's Art* that writing "comes in grades of quality in the fashion of beer and baseball games: good, better, and best" (Kansas City and New York: Andrews, McNeel & Parker, 1984, p. 11).

The purpose of *The Practical Writer's Guide* is to arm you with as many facts and guidelines as possible to help you progress successfully along *your* chosen scale. The benefits of such progress are enormous to business people, writers, students—everyone. People in the working world, especially, know that better communication means greater success in their careers; in many cases, effective communication is crucial to success. That's why so many people turn to books on writing for help.

Books on writing often deal with similar topics, but in many cases that's where the similarity ends. The *format* in this book, for instance, consists of many tables, lists, charts, and other illustrations without the usual text discussion. With this arrangement of information, vast amounts of essential data have been condensed into brief, quick-scan, easy-to-remember words, phrases, and statements. Any necessary supplementary data or commentary has been relegated to the position of abbreviated footnotes. With this format, more information could be included in the five chapters: "Writing Style and Techniques," "Elements of Grammar," "Contemporary Correspondence," "Manuscript Preparation and Production," and "Reference Section." The bottom line is that you get more for your money, thanks to the condensed format. The other bonus is that essential facts can be plucked from an abbreviated presentation shorn of excess verbiage more quickly and easily than from a traditional text discussion.

The decision to prepare a writing book in a condensed format came easily, especially since the subject of writing is a natural for any format based upon economy of words. This is one profession where *less* is often *better*. Also, a comprehensive writing book has to cover a lot of territory concerning grammar, usage, techniques, and procedures. That requisite means that one has to provide many rules and guidelines—prescriptions that are perfectly suited for an abbreviated format.

However important rules and guidelines may be—and they are unquestionably indispensable—finding access to them in books such as this one is only half of the battle. To know all of the dos and don'ts is certainly praiseworthy, but to be able to translate these various gems into good (better, best) writing is the ultimate victory. Since the scramble to earn a living forces us to take this dictum seriously, *The Practical Writer's Guide* offers the other necessary dimension in a basic writing reference work: models and examples. To satisfy our inherent desire to visualize and imitate—and deal with the constant pressure to save time and effort in a busy world—this book has an abundance of illustrations such as the examples of trite expressions in Chapter 1 and the model letters and memos in Chapter 3.

We all rely on both examples and rules in our writing, but only a masochist would want to memorize all of the rules in this or any other reference book—and the key word is *reference*.

—Imagine that you are writing an article and can't remember whether the past tense of *shrink* is *shrank* or *shrunk*. Teachers tell us that most students would miss a question about that on a quiz, and the rest of us would not do much better. However, in a few seconds you can glance at the list **COMMON IRREGULAR VERBS** in Chapter 2, and you will see that either one is correct.

—You may be writing a letter and are wondering whether your reference line should be typed above or below the dateline. A quick look at the model letters and the instructions in **PRINCIPAL PARTS OF LETTERS** in Chapter 3 will tell you that it goes two lines below the dateline or any notation following the dateline.

—Perhaps it is your job to prepare a company news bulletin, and you have been told to type one column twenty picas wide for page 1 and another column forty picas wide for page 2. But how many *inches* do you mark off on your typing paper? You can find the answer merely by glancing at the table **PICAS AND EQUIVALENT INCHES** in Chapter 5: twenty picas equals about 3.3 or 3⁵⁄₁₆ inches, and forty picas, therefore, equals about 6.6 or 6¹⁰⁄₁₆ inches. If you have no idea what a pica is, turn to the Glossary.

Like any easy-access source book, this one is meant to be used to look up information—in this case, information you need to write more accurately, easily, and skillfully or, as some might stress, to improve the *quality* of your writing.

Although the information that writers need often goes beyond the basic elements of composition and grammar to related areas such as typesetting and printing, most writing books ignore the production aspect of writing. Yet many people in the working world must also edit, typemark, and proofread their written material; type their drafts; prepare an index; and arrange for typesetting, printing, and copyright. To fill the large gap in information about these tasks, Chapters 4 and 5 include information on these subjects.

Some areas should be of concern to all writers. But in spite of the so-called enlightened and liberated culture of the 1980s, handicapped persons, women, and people of black, Hispanic, Asian, and other heritages are still being humiliated and insulted on paper every day. Chapter 1, therefore, covers another often neglected topic—nondiscriminatory writing.

Other sections throughout the book reflect a more positive aspect of modern society, namely, the technological revolution. "Contemporary Abbreviations" in Chapter 5, for example, includes common computer abbreviations, and "Manuscript-Preparation Guidelines" in Chapter 4 includes preparation of material by computer or word processor.

The selected topics in *The Practical Writer's Guide* are as much a distillation of a larger collection of topics as the tables and lists are a condensed version of a wider text discussion. Deciding which topics to include was the most difficult part of writing this book. But I had a lot of good advice, and I want to thank my writer, editor, and teacher colleagues for helping me set my sights in the right direction and for sending me useful letters, articles, reference lists, and other material. I especially want to thank Richard Balkin of the Balkin Agency and Hugh Rawson of New American Library, who were the first to recognize the value of a condensed format for this book when my concept was still in an embryonic stage. Perhaps they knew that Thoreau had the right idea back in 1854 (remember *Walden*?): "Our life is frittered away by detail. . . . Simplify, simplify."

1. WRITING STYLE AND TECHNIQUES

How you say something, your writing style, tells others more about you than you can imagine. It reveals the level of your writing skill and your attention to details such as accuracy and consistency. Your remarks are a mirror that reflects your attitude and ability to communicate effectively, an image that makes an indelible impression upon recipients. Where writing is concerned, it is much easier to learn how to do it right than to undo the damage of doing it wrong. Since the consequences of faulty communication can be so severe, ongoing attention to writing style and techniques should be a high-priority goal of every individual.

BASIC STEPS IN THE WRITING PROCESS

ORGANIZATION

Plan ahead; decide what steps are required to begin your project (for example, prepare a questionnaire; arrange for telephone and personal interviews; write for books and other printed materials; develop an outline; purchase supplies; select databases, libraries, and other research facilities) and put the steps in proper sequence.

Define your thesis and objective. Briefly summarize (in writing) what you want your message to accomplish, to whom it will be directed (audience), and how much information you want to convey (depth and detail).

Organize your research and writing tools (for example, tape recorder, modem, camera, index cards and notebooks, typing or word-processing supplies) and develop a checklist of things to do. Check off each step as you complete it.

RESEARCH

Build upon the initial organizational stage; define (in writing) what information you need and determine where to find it (for example, libraries, professional clubs and associations, company files, government agencies, personal interviews). Estimate the cost of the information (for example, books and other printed material; film; tapes; computer-research, art, and photography services), how long it will take to secure it (the telephone is a convenient timesaving device in fact finding), and the most efficient way to record it (for example, cassette, diskette, index cards, questionnaires, notebooks). Schedule interview appointments and place orders for publications and supplies immediately to avoid delays.

Convert your brief thesis-objective summary into an orderly list of one- or two-word major topics. Under each major topic write as many subtopics (and sub-subtopics) as you can. After you start reading, interviewing, and note taking, expand, revise, and refine your research-topic list as often as necessary.

Keep notes on each topic and subtopic on separate sheets of paper or index cards so that you can easily reshuffle them (change the order of your topics). Record each bibliography source on a separate index card for easy alphabetizing. Record sources of information as you take notes to insure proper footnoting of quoted material (request permission to use copyrighted material and use release forms in interviewing and picture taking; see **RELEASE FORMS** in Chapter 5). Record more information than you need so that you can be selective in the drafting stage.

DRAFTING

Prepare your first draft by expanding upon the research-topic list. Convert each one- or two-word topic and subtopic into a complete sentence. See **TOPIC AND SENTENCE OUTLINES** in this chapter. Review the order of topics again and rearrange them as needed. Expand each sentence into a paragraph and each paragraph into a section, or group of paragraphs. Do not worry about writing style, correct spelling, or other refinements now, but do record quoted material carefully and state sources (for footnotes) as you write.

Place footnotes at the bottom of each page with quoted material or collect them in a notes section at the end of your manuscript. If you want original photographs and graphics, rather than reprints, you may need to hire a photographer and a commercial artist (or an agency) to prepare them. Position tables, photographs, charts, and so on at the proper place in the text or collect them at the end of the manuscript (refer to each item in your text discussion; for example, "see Figure 3").

Double-check the manuscript for completeness and locate any missing information. Prepare the front matter (title page, table of contents, and so on; see Chapter 4).

REVISION

Evaluate what you have written and verify facts and figures. Review the sequence of topics and rearrange sentences, paragraphs, and sections as needed. Check the position of footnotes, bibliography, and illustrations. Polish the beginning (it must immediately hook readers and move them into the body without delay) and the end (it must bring your discussion to a logical conclusion and not leave readers hanging).

Check the smoothness of transition from sentence to sentence and paragraph to paragraph. One should slide into another, without a sudden shift or clumsy, jerky movement in thought and words. Examine your writing to be certain the tone and language are appropriate for the audience and that your ideas are clear, relevant, and well documented. Eliminate wordiness and rambling. Check grammar, consistency in capitalization and punctuation, correct word choice, spelling, and so on. See **EDITING CHECKLIST** in Chapter 4.

Put the draft aside—overnight if possible—and return to it later. Continue to rewrite and polish it as many times as necessary. Refer to the various techniques and procedures described in Chapters 1–4; see also **INDEX-PREPARATION PROCEDURES** in Chapter 4.

TOPIC AND SENTENCE OUTLINES

Topic Outline	*Sentence Outline*
I. Essential steps in successful writing	Four essential steps in successful writing are (a) getting organized, (b) conducting research, (c) preparing drafts, and (d) revising rough copy.
(a) Organization	The first step in a writing project should consist primarily of planning and organizational activities.
(b) Research	Research is the process of gathering and recording information.
(c) Drafting	A good way to start a draft is to expand your topic outline into a sentence outline.
(d) Revision	Successful writers may check, correct, and polish their rough drafts many times before they are satisfied.

NOTE: The conversion process illustrated here—topics expanded into sentences—can be continued, with sentences expanded into paragraphs, paragraphs expanded into sections, and sections expanded into chapters.

TRITE EXPRESSIONS

Trite	*Preferred*
This will *acknowledge receipt of* your manuscript.	We *received* your manuscript.
Allow me to express our appreciation for your report.	*Thank you for* your report.
We have your synopsis *at hand*.	We received your synopsis.
Yours of the 10th received and *contents carefully noted*.	The suggestions in your October 10 memo will be on the agenda for our next meeting.
We received your *esteemed favor* of the 27th.	Thank you for your *letter* of January 27.
I *have before me* your revised manuscript.	*Thank you for* your revised manuscript.
We are *in receipt of* your index.	*Thank you for* your index.
Permit me to say that I appreciate your advice.	I appreciate your advice.
We received your check of *recent date*.	We received your *December 1, 1985*, payment.
Replying to yours of the 11th, I have the catalog you requested.	*Thank you for your letter* of July 11; the catalog you requested is enclosed. *Or:* Here is the catalog you requested.
Thank you kindly for the invitation to speak at your meeting.	*Thank you* for the invitation to speak at your meeting.

Trite	*Preferred*
Thank you for your *valued* order.	Thank you for your order.
Thank you for *yours of recent date*.	Thank you for *your order of August 2, 1985*.
Please return the enclosed checklist *at your convenience*.	Please return the enclosed checklist *by Monday, June 15, 1985*.
Enclosed please find our latest price list.	*Enclosed is* our latest price list.
I am enclosing my article "Witchcraft" *for your consideration*.	I am enclosing my article "Witchcraft."
A style sheet is enclosed *for your information*.	A style sheet is enclosed.
We *herewith hand you* a copy of our wastewater proposal.	*Enclosed is* a copy of our wastewater proposal.
I am attaching *hereto* the guidelines you requested.	Here are the guidelines you requested.
Enclosed *herewith* is your copy of the contract.	Enclosed is your copy of the contract.
Here are my recommendations *in re* the photo layout.	Here are my recommendations *for* the photo layout.
Enclosed is our check *in the amount of* $61.98.	Enclosed is our check *for* $61.98.
Kindly send the following items *and oblige*.	Please send the following items immediately.
I'd like your answer *as soon as possible*.	I'd like your answer *by Wednesday, April 9, 1985*.

Trite	*Preferred*
Awaiting your favor, I remain,	*I hope to hear from you soon.*
Thanking you in advance for any information you may have.	*I would appreciate* any information you may have.
The undersigned will appreciate any suggestions you may have.	*I* will appreciate any suggestions you may have.
This letter is for the purpose of inviting your comments.	Your comments will be welcome. *Or:* Please send us your comments.
I'd like to *advise* you about our new program.	I'd like to *tell* you about our new program.
After giving due consideration to each submission, we have made a decision.	*After considering* each submission, we have made a decision.
I plan to speak *along these lines.*	I plan to discuss *word processing for authors.*
The outline has been set up *as per* your instructions.	The outline has been set up *according to* your instructions.
I *beg to inform you that* we are no longer reading unsolicited manuscripts.	We are no longer reading unsolicited manuscripts.
Your order has been *duly* forwarded to our shipping department.	We have sent your order to our shipping department.
Please be advised that the deadline is Tuesday, February 7, 1985.	The deadline is Tuesday, February 7, 1985.

Trite	*Preferred*
The envelopes you ordered are being printed now. We will ship *same* on May 16, 1985.	The envelopes you ordered are being printed now. We will ship *them* on May 16, 1985.
I'll *state* our decision in my report.	I'll *tell you* our decision in my report.
We *take pleasure in* announcing the appointment of James Dawson as director.	We *are happy to* announce the appointment of James Dawson as director.
We regret to inform you that this book is out of stock.	*We are sorry* that this book is out of stock.
I would say that the title is appealing.	The title is appealing.
You claim that you sent us your remittance on November 18, 1985.	We are sorry that your remittance of November 18, 1985, never reached us.
We are happy to hear from you *at all times*.	We are *always* happy to hear from you.
We would like to begin processing *at this time*.	We would like to begin processing *now*.
We are ahead of schedule *at the present writing*.	We are ahead of schedule *now*.
Sales have been numerous *up to this writing*.	Sales have been numerous *until now*.
I will go by plane *in the event that* the weather is good.	I will go by plane *if* the weather is good.
This writer reached the same conclusion.	*I* reached the same conclusion.

Trite	*Preferred*
The company will introduce its new *line* in September.	The company will introduce its new *line of goods* in September.
Our Miss Jones will represent us at the fair.	*Ms. Jones* will represent us at the fair.
The newsstand price is $2 *per* issue.	The newsstand price is $2 *an* issue.
The possibilities are *too numerous to mention*.	The possibilities are *numerous*.

NOTE: See also **PRETENTIOUS LANGUAGE** in this chapter.

PRETENTIOUS LANGUAGE

Pretentious	*Preferred*
abate, abatement	cut down, decrease, drop
aggregation	total
approximately	about
assistance	aid, help
behest	request
bona fide	genuine
chef d'oeuvre	masterpiece
chemotherapeutic agent	drug
cognizant	aware
commence, inaugurate, initiate	begin, start
commendation	praise
commercialization	commerce
construct	make

Pretentious	*Preferred*
customary channels	usual way
delineate	describe, draw
dialogue	conversation
disseminate, promulgate	circulate, send out
domicile	home
effected, effectuated	made, did
endeavoring	trying
equivalent	equal
facilitate	ease, help
feedback	comments
forward, transmit	send
functionalization	use
germane	relevant
hiatus	gap, interval
impair	damage, hurt, weaken
in toto	altogether, in all
input	advice
instantaneously	now, quickly
instrumentalities	means, ways
interface with	meet with
involving, concerning	about
ipso facto	by the very nature of the case
lethal	deadly, fatal
milieu	surroundings, environment
modus operandi	method
multitudinous	many
nadir	low point
obfuscate	confuse
obviate	prevent, do away with
palpable	clear, obvious, visible
per annum	a year, each year
per diem	a day, each day
per se	as such
peruse	read
procedural practices	what to do and how to do it

Pretentious	*Preferred*
raison d'être	reason for
remuneration	pay
sine qua non	essential
succumbed	died
terminate	end
utilize, utilization	use
vicissitude	change
wherewithal	means

NOTE: Some expressions such as *interface* are appropriate in specific technical or professional contexts (for example, computers) but are pretentious when used in general writing. To avoid pretentious language, select shorter, simpler words (*home*) rather than long, more complex ones (*domicile*); use basic English words (*genuine*) rather than latinate terms (*bona fide*); and choose single-syllable words (*help*) rather than multisyllable ones (*facilitate*). See also **TRITE EXPRESSIONS** and **WORD-ECONOMY CHART** in this chapter.

DICTIONARY OF CORRECT WORD CHOICE

a while/awhile

A while, a noun phrase, refers to a period or interval. (Let's wait for *a while* and see if the rain stops.)

Awhile, an adverb, means "for a short time." (We should work *awhile* before leaving.) Do not use *for* with *awhile* since *for* is implied.

adapt/adept/adopt

Adapt means "to change something for one's own purposes; to adjust." (I *adapted* the meter to our console.)

Adept means "proficient, skilled." (She is *adept* in foreign languages.)

Adopt means "to accept something without changing it." (They *adopted* the resolutions.)

affect/effect

Affect, a verb, means "to influence." (How will this policy *affect* our schedule?)

Effect, as a noun, means "a result." (What *effect* did the speech have on the audience?) As a verb, it means "to bring about." (The new policy will *effect* better customer relations.)

aid/assist/help

Aid means "to provide relief or assistance" and suggests incapacity or helplessness on the part of the recipient. (The government provided *aid* to flood victims.)

Assist means "to support or aid" and suggests a secondary role. (Her staff will *assist* in the presentation.)

Help means "to assist; to promote; to relieve; to benefit," and suggests steps toward some end. (He *helped* them move the machine.)

all right/alright

All right means "safe; acceptable; yes." (The schematic looks *all right* to me.)

Alright is a misspelling of *all right*.

although/though

Although means "regardless; even though." It is preferred over *though* at the beginning of a sentence. (*Although* the plan failed we learned a lot from the experience.)

Though means the same thing but is used more to link words and phrases in the middle of a sentence. (It is true, *though*, that the index is too high.)

among/between

Among refers to the relationship of more than two things. (The exchange of opinions *among* the participants was hostile.)

Between refers to the relationship of two things or more than two things if each one is individually related to the others. (The exchange of opinions *between* Smith and Wright was hostile.)

anxious/eager

Anxious refers to uneasiness or worry. (I am *anxious* to know the outcome of the surgery.)

Eager suggests earnest desire or anticipation. (I am *eager* to start my new job.)

apt/liable/likely

Apt means "fit" (*apt* in journalism) or "inclined to do something" (*apt* to come early).

Liable means "obligated by law; responsible." (The company is *liable* if an accident occurs on the property.)

Likely means "probable." (An economic slowdown is *likely*.)

as/since

As is a less effective conjunction than *since*, but it has other uses in the English language: preposition, adverb, and pronoun.

Since (or *because, when*) is more effective and is preferred. (*Since* this issue is late, we will have to reschedule the next issue.)

as . . . as/so . . . as

As . . . as is preferred for positive expressions. (The next conference will be *as* successful *as* the last one.)

So . . . as is often preferred, but not essential, for negative expressions. (The revised proposal is not *so* good *as* the original version.)

as if/as though/like

As if is less formal than *as though*. (She hesitated to begin the project *as if* she were afraid it would fail.)

As though is used in the same sense, and like *as if*, it is followed by a verb in the subjunctive mood. (He angrily rejected the proposal *as though* it were a personal affront.)

Like is widely used and misused in informal conversation

(*like* I said), but authorities still recommend that it be used as a preposition and with a noun or pronoun that is *not* followed by a verb. (The president acts *like* a dictator.)

assure/ensure/insure

Assure means "to guarantee." It is used only in reference to persons. (I can *assure* you that we intend to complete the job on schedule.)

Ensure, a less common variation of *insure*, means "to make certain." (This long-range policy will *ensure* our continuing success.)

Insure, the preferred spelling of *ensure*, means "to make certain; to guard against risk or loss." (The mail room will *insure* the package.)

balance/remainder

Balance refers to a degree of equality (we want to *balance* the budget) or to bookkeeping (please double-check the *balance* in our account).

Remainder should be used in all other instances to mean "what is left over." (Five hundred of the 1,000 brochures were mailed this morning, and the *remainder* are almost ready for mailing now.)

barely/hardly/scarcely

Barely means "meagerly; narrowly." (He could *barely* fit into the small foreign car.)

Hardly means "with difficulty." (She could *hardly* control the car in the driving rain.)

Scarcely means "by a narrow margin" and suggests something hard to believe. (He could *scarcely* believe his application was rejected.)

Do not use a negative with any of these terms, since each already has a negative quality (*not:* not barely, not hardly, or not scarcely).

because/due to

Because should be used with nonlinking verbs. (They took the bus *because* their car was in the garage.)

Due to means "caused by" and may be used following a linking verb. (Their exhaustion was *due to* overwork.) *Due to* is often used by careless business writers as a wordy substitute for *since* or *because*.

capital/capitol

Capital means "a stock or value of goods." (The company needed more *capital* to expand.) It also means "the city that is the seat of government." (Concord is the *capital* of New Hampshire.)

Capitol refers to a state or the federal government building. It is always capitalized in reference to the seat of the United States Congress. (The *Capitol* in Washington, D.C., is a magnificent structure.)

close/near

Close means "very near" (*close* race) or "intimate" (*close* friend).

Near means "closely related" (*near* neighbors) or "narrow margin" (a *near* victory).

compare/contrast

Compare means "to examine for difference or similarity, mostly similarity." *Compare* is followed by *with* when specifics are examined. (She *compared* her record with his.) But in a general reference, *compare* is followed by *to*. (*Compared* to yesterday, today is tranquil.)

Contrast means "to show only differences." The noun form of *contrast* is followed by *to*. (The new typewriters have correcting features, in *contrast to* the old models.) But the verb *contrast* is usually followed by *with*. (His present position *contrasts* markedly *with* his old one.)

complement/compliment

Complement means "to complete." (The new study *complements* the previous report.)

Compliment means "to flatter or praise." (His employer *complimented* him on his achievement.)

compose/comprise

Compose means "to make up by combining." (Seven rooms *compose* the suite. *Or:* The suite is *composed* of seven rooms.) A general rule is that the parts (seven rooms) *compose* the whole (the suite).

Comprise means "to include." (The company *comprises* two hundred employees.) A general rule is that the whole (the company) *comprises* the parts (the employees).

continual/continuous

Continual means "always going on; repeated over and over," and often implies a steady or rapid succession. (The company is *continually* seeking part-time help.)

Continuous means "connected; unbroken; going on without interruption." (The computer is in *continuous* operation, day and night.)

convince/persuade

Convince means "to lead someone to understand, agree, or believe." (She *convinced* her employer that funding was inadequate.)

Persuade means "to win someone over." (I *persuaded* him to take the day off.)

currently/presently

Currently means "the time now passing; belonging to the present time." (The company is *currently* being formed.)

Presently means "shortly or before long." (She will arrive *presently*.)

deduction/induction

Deduction refers to reasoning by moving from the general to the particular. (All computers accept some form of symbolic data; therefore, the XL100 should accept symbolic input.)

Induction refers to reasoning by moving from the particular to the general. (Having read thousands of business letters, most of which have one or more grammatical errors, I believe that most business people need further education in basic English composition.)

defer/delay/postpone

Defer means "to put off something until later." (He *deferred* his decision until next week.)

Delay means "to set aside; to detain; to stop." (Let's *delay* further work on that project.)

Postpone means "to put off something until later, with full intention of undertaking it at a specific time." (The director *postponed* the meeting until Wednesday, October 6.)

different from/different than/different to

Different from is preferred by careful business writers. (My objective is *different from* yours.)

Different than is sometimes used when followed by a clause. (The results were *different than* he had expected they would be.)

Different to is a form of British usage.

differentiate/distinguish

Differentiate means "to show in detail a difference in." (You can *differentiate* among the paper samples by weight and grain.)

Distinguish also means "to show the difference in" but is used to point out general differences that separate one category from another. (You can easily *distinguish* radios from television sets.)

disinterested/uninterested

Disinterested means "objective, free from selfish motive; unbiased." (The researchers remained *disinterested* while making their survey.)

Uninterested means "indifferent, not interested." (He was *uninterested* in the new office decor.)

dissatisfied/unsatisfied

Dissatisfied means "unhappy; upset; displeased." (She is *dissatisfied* with her new position.)

Unsatisfied means "not content, not pleased; wanting something more or better to be done." (The supervisor was *unsatisfied* with the quality of the work.)

doubt if/doubt that/doubt whether

Doubt if should be avoided in business writing.

Doubt that is the preferred expression in negative or interrogative sentences when little doubt exists. (I *doubt that* we can meet the deadline.)

Doubt whether is usually limited to situations involving strong uncertainty. (I *doubt whether* anything will come of it.)

each other/one another

Each other is used when referring to two persons or objects. (The two attorneys consulted *each other* before taking action.)

One another is used when referring to three or more persons or objects. (The six candidates were debating with *one another* off camera as well as on camera.)

emigrate/immigrate

Emigrate means "to move from one place to another." (Feldman *emigrated* from Israel last year.)

Immigrate means "to enter a country to establish permanent residence." (O'Connell *immigrated* to the United States this spring.)

essentially/substantially

Essentially is used most often to mean "basically." (The new copier is *essentially* the same as the old one.) The word *essential* implies something indispensable. (Insurance is *essential*.)

Substantially is used in the same way to mean "basically," but the word *substantial* suggests a significant size or quantity. (The company showed a *substantial* net gain.)

farther/further

Farther refers to physical distance or spatial measurement. (Salespersons travel *farther* today, thanks to readily available air service.)

Further refers to quantity or degree. (This roll of film will go *further* than I expected.) It also means "to promote." (He hopes to *further* his career.) Some business writers have stopped distinguishing between *farther* and *further* and are using only one of them (usually *further*) for all situations.

feasible/possible

Feasible means "capable of being done." (The suggestion sounds *feasible* to me.)

Possible means "within realistic limits; likely to occur." (An economic upturn next quarter is *possible*.)

frequent/recurring

Frequent means "habitual; persistent; occurring at short intervals." (He is a *frequent* customer.)

Recurring means "occurring again and again; occurring repeatedly." (Her *recurring* headache suggests a serious problem.)

handle/manage

Handle means "to control or manage; to deal with," and is preferred over *manage* when physical action is involved. (He *handled* the controls like an expert.)

Manage also means "to control or handle; to deal with," and is preferred over *handle* when nonphysical action is involved. (She *managed* the office efficiently.)

happen/occur/transpire

Happen means "to occur by chance." (He *happened* to be in the neighborhood.)

Occur means "to take place, often unexpectedly," and usually refers to a specific event. (The computer breakdown *occurred* before closing.)

Transpire means "to pass off; to excrete as a vapor." (The leaves *transpired*). Figuratively, it means "to become apparent." (The state of the company became clear as events *transpired*.)

if/whether

If is used to introduce one condition and often suggests doubt. (I'll meet you at the airport *if* the weather permits.)

Whether is used to introduce more than one condition. (Her client asked *whether* she should sue or accept the settlement.)

imply/infer

Imply means "to suggest by inference or association." (The report *implies* that research was inadequate.)

Infer means "to reach a conclusion from facts or circumstances." (The manager *inferred* from the report that research was inadequate.)

impracticable/impractical/unpractical

Impracticable means "not capable of being used or accomplished." (The plan is *impracticable*.)

Impractical means "not capable of dealing sensibly or practically with something." (Her approach is *impractical*.)

Unpractical is an obsolete term for *impracticable*.

ineffective/ineffectual

Ineffective means "not producing the intended effect; not effective," and often suggests incompetence in some particular area. (He is *ineffective* as a salesman.)

Ineffectual also means "not producing the intended effect; not effective," and often suggests a general lack of competence. (He is *ineffectual*.)

know/realize

Know means "to perceive; to understand." (I *know* a better route.)

Realize means "to accomplish; to grasp fully," and implies a more thorough understanding than *know*. (I *realize* the implications of our action.)

lack/need/want

Lack, as a noun, means "deficiency or absence." (The program suffers from a *lack* of money.)

Need, as a noun, refers to "a lack of something desirable or useful" and often is used in an emotional context. (The *need* was for security.)

Want, as a noun, refers to "a lack of something needed or desired." (My *wants* seem to increase with age.)

As verbs, *lack* suggests a deficiency; *need,* a necessity; and *want,* a desire.

lawful/legal

Lawful means "in harmony with some form of law; rightful, ethical." (The directors considered the *lawful* implications of the amendment.)

Legal means "founded on the law; established by law." (The lottery is *legal* in New Hampshire.)

one's self/oneself

One's self is used less often than *oneself,* except when the emphasis is on the *self.* (Psychologists say *one's self* is an amazing entity to be explored endlessly.)

Oneself is the preferred spelling in most general usage. (One has to discipline *oneself* in any position.)

part/portion/share

Part means "a subdivision of the whole." (This is one *part* of the proposal.)

Portion means "a part or share of something usually intended for a specific purpose." (This *portion* of the program is reserved for questions and answers.)

Share means "the part or portion of something belonging to or given by someone." (His *share* of the estate is being held in trust.)

persons/people

Persons is often preferred in references to a few individuals or when specific individuals are being discussed. (The president and the treasurer were the only *persons* there from the board.)

People is often preferred in references to large groups or indefinite numbers. (The *people* from Eastern cultures sometimes find it difficult to adjust to Western ways.)

practical/practicable

Practical means "sensible; useful; realistic." (He used a *practical* approach to the problem.)

Practicable means "usable; feasible." (It simply is not *practicable* to complete the project in two weeks.)

presumably/supposedly

Presumably means "taken for granted; reasonably assumed to be true." (*Presumably* he is correct, since he ran all of the required tests.)

Supposedly means "believed, sometimes mistakenly, to be true; imagined to be true." (The order to halt production *supposedly* came from someone in the executive offices.)

principal/principle

Principal, as a noun, means "chief participant or head" (the *principal* in the lawsuit) or "a sum of money" (the mortgage payment including the *principal* and interest). As an adjective, it means "most important or consequential" (the *principal* reason).

Principle, a noun, means "a rule, doctrine, or assumption" (the *principle* of universal sovereignty).

proved/proven

Proved is the past tense of *prove*. (They *proved* their contention.)

Proven is an adjective (the *proven* method) and a past participle. (The volunteers have *proven* their loyalty.)

Proved is preferred. (The volunteers have *proved* their loyalty.)

reaction/reply/response

Reaction means "a response to stimuli." (The injection caused a violent *reaction*.) It should not be used to mean "attitude, viewpoint, feeling, or response."

Reply means "a response in words." (She sent her *reply* by messenger.)

Response is "a reply; an answer." (The client's *response* was positive.)

shall/will

Shall, traditionally, is used in the first person to express future time. (I *shall* be happy to go.) Some authorities believe *shall* sounds stuffy and snobbish and prefer to use *will*.

Will, traditionally, is used in the second or third person to express future time. (He *will* be happy to go.) Contemporary usage shows an increasing preference for *will* in all instances. (I *will*, you *will*, he/she *will*, they *will*.)

that/which

That refers to persons, animals, or things and should be used in restrictive clauses where the clause introduced by *that* is essential to explain the preceding information. (A company *that* has high standards is admired by the public.) The clause "that has high standards" provides essential information, since it is not enough to say "A company is admired by the public." Therefore, the clause should *not* be set off with commas.

Which refers to animals and things and should be used in nonrestrictive clauses where the clause introduced by *which* is not essential for the reader to understand the meaning of the other information in the sentence. (His company, *which* has high standards, is admired by the public.) The clause "which has high standards" provides additional information, but it is not essential for the reader to understand the statement "His company is admired by the public." Therefore, the clause *should* be set off with commas.

varied/various

Varied means "diverse; with numerous forms." (The logos on business letterheads are *varied*.)

Various means "dissimilar; separate; different." (The memo was sent to *various* divisions in the company.)

viable/workable

Viable means "capable of existence." (The new company is a *viable* entity.)

Workable means "practicable; feasible; capable of working or succeeding." (The plan seems *workable* to me.)

Source: Adapted from Mary A. De Vries, "Guide to Correct Word Choice," *Guide to Better Business Writing* (Piscataway, N.J.: New Century Publishers, 1981), 44–72. Used with permission.

WORD-ECONOMY CHART

Phrase (Preferred Short Form)	*Word Economy (Savings)*
a great deal of (much)	3
a majority of (most)	2
a number of (about)	2
accounted for by (due to, caused by)	1
add the point that (add that)	2
advise and inform (advise, *or* inform)	2
along the line of (like)	3
an example of this is the fact that (for example)	6
another aspect of the situation to be considered is (as for)	7
appraise and determine (determine, *or* appraise)	2
are of the opinion that (think that)	3
as regards (for, about)	1
as related to (for, about)	2
as to (about)	1
at a later date (later)	3
at a time when (when)	3
at the present writing (now)	3
based on the fact that (because)	4
chemotherapeutic agent (drug)	1
close proximity (proximity, near)	1

Phrase (Preferred Short Form)	*Word Economy (Savings)*
collect together (collect)	1
concerning the nature of (about)	3
deeds and actions (deeds, *or* actions)	2
depressed socioeconomic area (slum)	2
due to the fact that (because)	4
during the time that (while)	3
except in a small number of cases (usually)	6
exhibit a tendency to (tend to)	2
few [many] in number (few [many])	2
final conclusion (conclusion, end)	1
first and foremost (first)	2
for the purpose of (for, to)	3
for the reason that (because)	3
from the point of view of (for)	5
future prospect (prospect)	1
have an input into (contribute to)	2
help and assist (help, *or* assist)	2
hopes and aspirations (hopes, *or* aspirations)	2
if at all possible (if possible)	2
in case, in case of (if)	1, 2
in close proximity (near)	2
in favor of (for, to)	2
in light of the fact that (because)	5
in order to (to)	2
in rare cases (rarely)	2
in [with] reference to, in regard to (about)	2
in relation with (with)	2
in terms of (in, for)	2
in the case of (regarding)	3
in the case that (if, when)	3
in the course of (during)	3

Phrase (Preferred Short Form)	*Word Economy (Savings)*
in the event that (if)	3
in the first place (first)	3
in the majority of instances (usually)	4
in the matter of (about)	3
in the nature of (like)	3
in the neighborhood of (about)	3
in the normal course of our procedure (normally)	6
in the not-too-distant future (soon)	5
in the opinion of this writer (in my opinion, I believe)	3, 4
in the vicinity of (near)	3
in view of the fact that (therefore)	5
inasmuch as (because)	1
involve the necessity of (require)	3
is defined as (is)	2
is dependent upon (depends on)	1
it is clear that (therefore, clearly)	3
it is observed that (*delete*)	4
it is often the case that (often)	5
it is our conclusion in light of investigation (we conclude that)	5
it should be noted that the . . . (the . . .)	5
it stands to reason (*delete*)	4
it was noted that if (if)	4
it would not be unreasonable to assume (I assume)	5
leaving out of consideration (disregarding)	3
make an examination of (examine)	3
marketing representative (salesperson)	1
mental attitude (attitude)	1
month of January (January)	2

Phrase (Preferred Short Form)	Word Economy (Savings)
mutual compromise (compromise)	1
not of a high order of accuracy (inaccurate)	6
notwithstanding the fact that (although)	3
of considerable magnitude (big, large, great)	2
of very minor importance (unimportant)	3
on account of the conditions described (because of the conditions)	2
on account of the fact that (because)	5
on a few occasions (occasionally)	3
on the grounds that (because)	3
out of (of)	1
outside [inside] of (outside [inside])	1
perform an analysis of (analyze)	3
personal friend (friend)	1
positive growth (growth)	1
prior to, in advance of (before)	1, 2
proceed to investigate (investigate)	2
prompt and speedy (prompt, quick, or speedy)	2
refer to as (call)	2
refuse and decline (refuse, or decline)	2
relative to this (about this)	1
renovate like new (renovate)	2
resultant effect (effect)	1
right and proper (right, or proper)	2
short minute (minute, moment)	1
solid facts (facts)	1
subsequent to (after)	1
successful triumph (triumph)	1

Phrase (Preferred Short Form)	Word Economy (Savings)
taking this factor into consideration, it is apparent that (therefore, therefore it seems)	8, 6
that is, i.e. (*avoid*)	2, 1
the bulk of (most)	2
the data show that . . . can (. . . can)	4
the existence of (*avoid*)	3
the foregoing (the, this, that, these, those)	1
the fullest possible (most, completely, fully)	2
the only difference being that (except)	4
the question as to whether (whether)	4
the year of 19— (19—)	3
there are not very many (few)	4
tire and fatigue (tire)	2
to be sure (of course, *or avoid*)	1, 3
to summarize the above (in sum, in summary)	2
with reference to (about)	2
with the exception of (except)	3
with the result that (so that)	2
with this in mind, it is clear that (therefore, clearly)	4, 3
within the realm of possibility (possible, possibly)	4

NOTE: Even when the word economy is not substantial, the short form is preferred. For example, although there is a savings of only one word, *conclusion* is preferred over *final conclusion*, which is redundant. See also **PRETENTIOUS LANGUAGE** in this chapter.

NONDISCRIMINATORY-WRITING GUIDELINES

Racial and Ethnic Discrimination

COLOR CLASSIFICATION

Rephrase classifications that divide people into white and nonwhite groups; identify the heritages.
Example: The company has a new policy regarding its black, Mexican-American, and Asian [*not:* nonwhite] apprentices.

UNDUE EMPHASIS

Omit words and phrases that perpetuate negative attitudes and draw attention to racial and ethnic backgrounds.
Example: Jerry Washington is a graduate [*not:* a black graduate] of Iowa State University.

HUMILIATION

Omit words that humiliate members of a racial or an ethnic group.
Example: The company's job-training program is directed toward black and Puerto Rican job applicants [*not:* disadvantaged minorities].

REVERSE IMPLICATION

Rephrase remarks that suggest that members of a particular group are the opposite.
Example: Rita Gonzolas is a skilled receptionist [*not:* an unusually well mannered receptionist, which might suggest that people of the same heritage are not usually well mannered].

STEREOTYPING

Avoid myths and comments that stereotype members of a racial or an ethnic group.

Example: Some people are clever and enterprising [*not:* Jews are clever and enterprising].

Handicap Bias

UNDUE EMPHASIS

Omit words and phrases that perpetuate negative attitudes and draw attention to a person's handicap; if reference to a disability is necessary, make it incidental.

Example: Adam Sloane, who is a paraplegic veteran [*not:* the paraplegic veteran Adam Sloane], will lecture to our class about careers for disabled veterans.

HUMILIATION

Rephrase negative, demeaning comments; use *seizure* instead of *fit*, *slow learner* instead of *retarded*, *disabled* or *handicapped* instead of *crippled*, *speech and hearing impaired* instead of *deaf and dumb*, *emotional difficulties* instead of *insanity*.

Example: The new training program has a special session for handicapped workers [*not:* cripples].

AVOIDANCE

Do not draw attention to a disability or make it worse by pretending it is insignificant or does not exist.

Example: Joe, perhaps you could help us devise a way for employees to maneuver wheelchairs through the cafeteria [*not:* Perhaps you would rather eat at your desk, Joe].

STEREOTYPING

Avoid myths and comments that stereotype people with handicaps.
Example: She has perfect hearing [*not:* She has extraordinary hearing ability since she is blind].

Sexism

ASEXUAL REFERENCES

Use asexual words such as *people* or *civilization* for *mankind, hours* for *man-hours, salesperson* for *salesman,* and *business people* for *businessmen.*
Example: It is one example in the history of civilization [*not:* mankind].

PARALLEL REFERENCES

Use first and last names and personal titles equally for men and women; use *Ms.* for a woman's title unless you know that she prefers *Miss* or *Mrs.* See **CONTEMPORARY FORMS OF ADDRESS** in Chapter 3.
Example: Mr. John Hill and Ms. Mary Watts [*not:* Mr. John Hill and Mary].

PERSONAL EMPHASIS

Do not substitute personal characteristics for professional capabilities in women, no matter how flattering the reference is intended to be.
Example: Representing the university were Henry Steinberg, director, and Joanne Johnson, assistant director [*not:* Henry Steinberg, director, and his attractive assistant Joanne].

AGE AND GENDER

Refer to adult males as men and adult females as women or use neutral terms such as *staff*.
Example: The men and women [*not:* men and girls] from our branch office toured the new facility.

SPOUSES

Use the neutral reference *spouse* in general situations.
Example: Registered guests and their spouses [*not:* wives] are invited to the banquet.

UNDUE EMPHASIS

Omit words and phrases that perpetuate negative attitudes and draw attention to a person's sex.
Example: The technician [*not:* woman technician] made some adjustments in the equipment.

MALE REFERENCE POINT

Do not use *his* as a general reference point; use *his and (or) her* or *their*.
Example: Each writer must choose his or her [*not:* his] specialty. *Or:* Writers must choose their own specialties.

ABBREVIATION GUIDELINES

GENERAL ABBREVIATIONS

Do not use general abbreviations in nontechnical writing, except in footnotes, tables, charts, invoices, and so on. *Example:* manager (*not:* mgr.); inch (*not:* in.)

SPECIALIZED FIELDS

In specialized areas, follow the style in your profession. *Example:* Law offices use the abbreviation *In re* (in regard to) to introduce a subject line in correspondence, but business offices use the word *Subject* spelled out.

CONSISTENCY

Be consistent in your use of abbreviations. *Example:* Chicago, Ill., and Boston, Mass. (*not:* Chicago, Ill., and Boston, Massachusetts)

CAPITALIZATION

The trend is toward the use of small (lowercase) letters, although some terms are still more familiar in capital (uppercase) letters. But follow the style in your profession. *Example:* fob (free on board); IQ (intelligence quotient)

PUNCTUATION

The trend is to omit periods, except when an abbreviation spells out an actual word that is not written in solid capitals; some abbreviations such as degrees and certain Latin abbreviations still use periods.

Example: YWCA; cm (centimeter); in. (for *inch* to distinguish from the word *in*); Sc.D.; op. cit.

Omit the period in short forms of words that are commonly used as complete words.
Example: memo (*not:* memo.)

Omit the period when a person is referred to by a letter of the alphabet.
Example: Mr. T (*not:* Mr. T.)

Omit the period after words written as contractions in informal writing.
Example: nat'l (*not:* nat'l.)

Omit the period after symbols reprenting chemical elements.
Example: H_2O (*not:* H_2O.)

Omit the period after a nickname, but use a period after an abbreviation of a first or middle name.
Example: Billy; Jas.

WORDS ALWAYS ABBREVIATED

Abbreviate titles, degrees, time designations, and other words that are widely accepted in abbreviated form.
Example: Mr.; Dr.; Ed.D.; a.m.; B.C.

Abbreviate *Jr., Sr.,* and *Esq.* after a personal name. (Some writers omit the comma before *Jr.* and *Sr.,* but one should retain it if the person prefers to have it included in his name.)
Example: Mr. Samuel Bernstein, Jr.; Evelyn Rogers, Esq.

COUNTRIES, STATES, GEOGRAPHIC PREFIXES, AND COMPASS POINTS

Spell out the names of most countries, although initials may be used as an adjective in some cases in informal writing.

Example: the United States; U.S. currency; the USSR; France (*not:* Fr.)

Spell out names of states in general writing; use traditional state abbreviations in footnotes, bibliographies, and so on; and use two-letter postal abbreviations in mailing addresses. *Example:* He is from New Mexico. Mail it to: 1411 East Avenue, New York, NY 10017. Boston, Mass.: Harvard University Press, 1981.

Spell out prefixes of geographic names in general writing. *Example:* Saint (*not:* St.) Lawrence

Abbreviate compass points after street names (no space). *Example:* 1904 Blueberry Drive, N.E.

DAYS AND MONTHS

Spell out days and months, except in tables, invoices, and so on. *Example:* January (*not:* Jan.)

ORGANIZATIONS

Spell out the name of an organization in informal writing at first mention followed by its initials in parentheses, except for especially well known names (use capital letters, no periods, and no space). *Example:* American Bar Association (ABA); CIA

Abbreviate *company* when it is part of an organization's official name and in footnotes and bibliographies. *Example:* Madison Leather Co. (actual name); the company; Cincinnati: ABC Printing Co., 1984.

ACRONYMS

Use well-known acronyms and popular abbreviations in informal writing without spelling them out the first time; some popular abbreviations, however, should be avoided even in informal writing.

Example: SALT; post office (*not:* PO)

CONTRACTIONS

Use an abbreviation instead of a contraction when a short form is permissible.

Example: dept. (*not:* dep't)

PROMINENT PERSONS

A few prominent persons may be referred to by initials in informal writing (no space and no periods).

Example: FDR; JFK; Ronald Reagan (*not:* RR)

TITLES

When *the* precedes religious, military, and honorary titles and when the titles precede a surname alone, spell them in full.

Example: The Reverend Edward Adams; Lieutenant McHenry; Col. Jane Oakes; Hon. Sidney Blackmore

LATIN TERMS

Some abbreviations are commonly used as short forms of Latin terms.

Example: ls for *locus sigilli* (place of the seal)

NOTE: For numerous examples of abbreviations, see **CONTEMPORARY ABBREVIATIONS** in Chapter 5.

SPELLING GUIDELINES

Plurals

SINGULAR NOUNS

Add *s* to form the plural of most singular nouns.
Example: house, houses; train, trains

COMPOUND NOUNS

Generally add *s* to the most important part of a compound noun. When a word ends in *-ful,* add *s* to the end of it.
Example: senators-elect; courthouses; cupfuls

IRREGULAR NOUNS

The plurals of some words are formed by a change in spelling, or they retain the same form in the plural.
Example: child, children; corps, corps

NOUNS ENDING IN *O*

When a word ends with a vowel followed by *o,* add *s.* When a word ends with a consonant followed by *o,* add *es* in most cases, *s* in a few cases, and either *s* or *es* in a few cases.
Example: studio, studios; hero, heroes; memo, memos; zēro, zeros, zeroes

NOUNS ENDING IN *Y*

When a word ends with a consonant followed by *y,* change the *y* to *i* and add *es.* When the *y* follows a vowel, add *s.*
Example: category, categories; attorney, attorneys

NOUNS ENDING IN *CH, SH, SS,* OR *X*

When a word ends in *ch, sh, ss,* or *x,* add *es.*
Example: church, churches; fish, fishes; glass, glasses; box, boxes

NOUNS ENDING IN *F, FF,* OR *FE*

When a word ends in *f, ff,* or *fe,* add *s* or change the *f* to *v* and add *es.* But no clear-cut rule exists to tell you when to change the *f* to *v.*
Example: proof, proofs; cliff, cliffs; safe, safes; *but:* shelf, shelves

Prefixes

PUNCTUATION

Write most prefixes closed (no hyphen).
Example: preestablished; selfsame; reform; *but:* anti-American; self-evident; re-form (to form again)

DOUBLE S

When a word begins with *s,* keep the *s* after adding the prefix *mis-* or *dis-.*
Example: spell, misspell; step, misstep

Suffixes and Verb Endings

WORDS THAT DOUBLE THE FINAL CONSONANT

When a one-syllable word ends with one vowel followed by one consonant, double the final consonant in most cases before adding a word ending starting with a vowel.
Example: drop, dropped; ship, shipped; *but:* bus, buses

When a multisyllable word ends with one vowel followed by one consonant and the accent falls on the last syllable, double the final consonant in most cases before adding a word ending starting with a vowel.
Example: control, controlling; regret, regrettable; *but:* prefer, preferable

WORDS THAT DO NOT DOUBLE THE FINAL CONSONANT

When a one-syllable word ends with one vowel followed by one consonant, do not double the final consonant before adding an *-ly* ending.
Example: glad, gladly; sad, sadly

When a multisyllable word ends with one vowel followed by one consonant and the accent does not fall on the last syllable, in most cases do not double the final consonant before adding a word ending starting with a vowel.
Example: travel, traveling; credit, credited; *but:* program, programming

When a multisyllable word ends with more than one vowel followed by a consonant, in most cases do not double the final consonant before adding a word ending.
Example: look, looking; appeal, appealing; *but:* equip, equipping

When a multisyllable word ends with more than one consonant, do not double the final consonant before adding a word ending.
Example: confirm, confirmed; element, elements

WORDS ENDING IN SILENT *E*

When a word ends with a silent *e*, drop the *e* in most cases before adding a word ending starting with a vowel.
Example: arrive, arrival; sale, salable; *but:* mile, mileage

When a word ends with a silent *e*, retain the *e* before a word ending that starts with a consonant unless another vowel precedes the final *e*.
Example: manage, management; argue, argument

WORDS ENDING IN *CE* OR *GE*

When a word ends in *ce* or *ge*, retain the *e* in most cases before adding a word ending that starts with *a*, *o*, or *u*.
Example: courage, courageous; notice, noticeable; *but:* age, aging

When a word ends in *ce* or *ge*, retain the final *e* before adding *-able* or *-ous*, but drop it before adding *-ible*.
Example: knowledge, knowledgeable; deduce, deducible.

WORDS WITH *IE*

When a word ends in *ie*, change the *ie* to *y* before adding *-ing*. In most cases, the rule for the order of *i* and *e* is "*i* before *e* except after *c* or when sounded like *a* as in *neighbor* and *weigh*."
Example: tie, tying; believe (*i* before *e*); receive (except after *c*); weight (when sounded like *a*)

WORDS ENDING IN *Y*

When a word ends in a consonant followed by *y*, change the *y* to *i* in most cases before all word endings except those starting with *i*.
Example: modify, modification; try, trying; *but:* dry, drier, dryer

When a word ends in a vowel followed by *y*, keep the *y* in most cases before adding a word ending.
Example: buy, buyer; employ, employment; *but:* day, daily

WORDS ENDING IN *-ATION*

When a word ends in *-ation*, change it to *-able*. No clear-cut rule exists for using *-able* and *-ible*.
Example: communication, communicable; application, applicable

WORDS ENDING IN *-IZE*, *-ISE*, AND *-YZE*

No rule exists in American usage for *-ize*, *-ise*, and *-yze*. Most words end in *-ize*, some in *-ise*, and a few in *-yze*. (British usage favors *-ise* over *-ize*.)
Example: summarize; compromise; analyze

WORDS ENDING IN *-ANCE*, *-ANCY*, AND *-ANT*

In most cases use *-ance*, *-ancy*, and *-ant* when a word has a *c* that sounds like *k* or has a *g* with a hard sound.
Example: extravagance; significant

WORDS ENDING IN *-ENCE*, *-ENCY*, AND *-ENT*

In most cases use *-ence*, *-ency*, and *-ent* when a word has a *c* that sounds like *s* or a *g* that sounds like *j*.
Example: convalescent; intelligence

WORDS ENDING IN *-SEDE*, *-CEED*, AND *-CEDE*

One word in English ends in *-sede;* three words end in *-ceed;* all others in this category end in *-cede.*
Example: supersede; proceed, exceed, succeed; recede, concede, precede

NOTE: Since numerous exceptions apply to many of the rules of spelling, consult a modern dictionary when in doubt.

CORRECT USE OF NUMBERS AND FRACTIONS

STANDARD RULES

Follow the style (no. 1 or 2) in your profession:

(1) Spell out the numbers one through ten, except in paragraphs also having larger numbers.
Example: two to three paragraphs; 10 to 11 guests; 68 to 70 employees; 100–200 books; 2 million copies; 2,000,000 copies printed and 1,791,643 sold

(2) Spell out numbers under one hundred as well as large round numbers such as two thousand, except in paragraphs having large uneven numbers.
Example: forty to fifty cartons; two hundred to three hundred cars; 0 to 101 chances; 17 million children; 4,361,090 adults and 17,000,000 children

INDEFINITE AMOUNTS

Spell out indefinite amounts
Example: several hundred dollars; more than a million spectators

BEGINNING OF A SENTENCE

Spell out numbers at the beginning of a sentence even when your style is to use figures elsewhere in the sentence. *Example:* Seven percent of the students fail, but 93 percent succeed.

NUMBERS AS NUMBERS

Use figures for numbers referred to as numbers. *Example:* add 8 and 9; nos. 4 and 5

PUNCTUATION

Separate adjacent numbers with a comma. *Example:* In 1985, 11 million employees changed jobs.

Enclose years in commas when both month and day are given with the year. *Example:* The manuscript is due on May 19, 1986, and I have four chapters to write.

Use an apostrophe and *s* in plural figures only if it might be confusing to omit the punctuation; form the plural of spelled-out numbers by adding *s* or *es*. *Example:* 1970s and 1980s; 5's and 6's; twos and threes; twenties and thirties

Use a decimal point consistently in a paragraph with numbers. *Example:* $121 and $149; $105.50 and $211.00; $6.68 and $0.19

DIVISION OF NUMBERS

Avoid dividing numbers; when they must be divided, separate the parts only at the comma. *Example:* 3,804,-690,000 (*not:* 3,80-4,690,000)

INCLUSIVE NUMBERS

Abbreviate numbers over one hundred that are joined by a hyphen unless the first number ends in two zeros, unless the second number starts with different digits, and when different centuries are represented.
Example: 1978–79; 1878–1979; 13–14; 183–84; 290–95; 100–105; 301–1088; 407–8 (*but: from* 407 *to* 408; *from* 541 *to* 542)

TIME AND DATE

Spell out nontechnical references to time, centuries, and decades; use figures for measures in technical material.
Example: nine hours; twentieth century; eighties; 9 cpm

Use figures with *a.m.* and *p.m.;* use the words *o'clock* and *half past* in formal writing.
Example: 7:30 p.m.; 11 a.m.; 6 o'clock (informal) or six o'clock (formal); half past seven o'clock (*not:* seven-thirty o'clock)

Write dates in general text writing and correspondence in a month-day-year sequence (the military and some other organizations use a day-month-year sequence, and this style is also used in footnotes and bibliographies).
Example: June 7, 1985 (*not:* June 7th or 6/7/85); 7 June 1985 (footnote and bibliography style)

ADDRESSES

Use figures in addresses for house and building numbers (but spell out the number one); spell out one through ten in street names. Use arabic numerals for highways.
Example: 271 East Boulevard; One Park Avenue; 785 Fifth Avenue; 1144 12th Street; U.S. Route 66

MONEY

Repeat the full amount in figure ranges involving dollars. Capitalize numbers in sums of money in checks.
Example: $2 million to $4 million (*not:* $2 to 4 million); Two Hundred Dollars ($200)

DOCUMENTS AND NAMES

Capitalize numbers in formal documents, in names or classifications with numbers, and in formal names containing numbers. Use arabic figures with unions and lodges.
Example: Eighty-ninth Congress; Third Reich; Local No. 14; American Legion Post No. 1105

FRACTIONS

Hyphenate fractions when the numerator and denominator are both one-word forms, but omit the hyphen when either the numerator or denominator already has a hyphen.
Example: one-fifth; one-hundredth; one forty-eighth; seventy-two twenty-fifths

RATIOS AND PROPORTIONS

Use numbers for ratios and proportions.
Example: 4:1 ratio; 1,000 to 1 odds; 50-50 chance

NOTE: See also **ARABIC AND ROMAN NUMERALS** in Chapter 5.

RULES OF PUNCTUATION

APOSTROPHE (')

Used to show possession, omission, and some plurals; omit it for plurals if *s* can stand alone without confusion.
Example: p's and q's; 4's and 5's; 1980s; YMCAs

To show *possession,* add an apostrophe and *s* to a singular word; omit *s* if the word already ends in *ss;* add an apostrophe alone to a plural word that already ends in *s.*
Example: publisher's employees; boss' idea; four days' work

With *names,* add an apostrophe and *s* to a singular word and an apostrophe alone to a plural word; use an apostrophe to distinguish between joint and separate possession.
Example: Carol Webster's house; the Adamses' party; Jim and George's proposal (joint); Jim's and George's proposals (separate)

To show *omission,* use an apostrophe in place of omitted letters and numbers.
Example: he'll (he will); '80s (1980s)

BRACKETS [ ]

Used around remarks and corrections that are not part of quoted material and to enclose parenthetical remarks within parentheses. No space between brackets and enclosed material.
Example: "Yes," he said, "the program for this year [1985] is at the printer." The publisher is increasing the number of titles this year (as he did last year [1984]).

COLON (:)

Used after letter salutations; to show ratios and time; to introduce a list, quotation, or example (do not use after verbs

such as *are* unless a formal listing follows); between dates
and pages and between cities and publishers in references;
and to indicate pause between two closely related sentences
not linked by a conjunction. Two spaces after a colon, except
no space when the colon directly links two numbers as in
clock time.

Example: Dear Ms. Margolis: 10:1 ratio; 11:45 p.m.;
the following parts: table of contents, foreword, and bibliography; *Digest* 3 (1983): 21-11; Boston: ABC Publishers, 1984;
The writer had one objective: she wanted to write children's
stories.

COMMA (,)

Used to separate three or more words or phrases in a series
(*series comma*) and clauses of a compound sentence and for
words omitted in a series. Set off *nonrestrictive* (nonessential) clauses, introductory and transitional words and phrases,
words in apposition, parenthetical expressions, and quoted
material. One space after a comma.

Example: pencil, paper, and eraser; Two writers worked on
the project last year; three, this year. The manuscript, which
has fourteen chapters, is ready for submission. When you've
finished, let me see the draft, please. Therefore, you must
wait. The editor, Ms. Willis, is here. "It's true," she said,
"that they made an offer." In January 1985, 2.5 million
workers relocated. A month earlier, they were optimistic.

DASH (—)

Used to show sudden interruption or to set off and emphasize
clauses of explanation. Do not use with other punctuation
marks in succession (*not:* "Now,—it is said—the real work
begins"). No space before or after a dash.

Example: Pencils, paper, typewriter—these are the tools of a writer. Her new desk—new to her, that is—has arrived. Money—who doesn't need it?

ELLIPSIS (. . .)

Used to show the omission of words: three dots, words omitted at the beginning or in the middle of a sentence; four dots, words, sentences, and paragraphs omitted at the end of a sentence. There are never more than four dots, even when the end of one sentence and the beginning of the next one are omitted. Generally, one space between dots. No space between end of sentence and dot that represents a period. For additional examples, see **USE OF QUOTED MATERIAL, Omission** and **Extracts**, in Chapter 4.
Example: According to my agent, "Sales increased . . . last year. . . . But a decline is expected next year."

EXCLAMATION POINT (!)

Used to show surprise, irony, or strong feeling (do not overuse). Two spaces after a sentence.
Example: Oh, no! They lost my manuscript! Hurry! The game is almost over! Order Today!

HYPHEN (-)

Used to divide words at the end of a line and to link compound words; in fractions; with prefixes before a proper name; and in various numbers such as telephone numbers. No space before or after a hyphen except after a suspended hyphen (two- to three-shelf unit). See also **RULES OF WORD DIVISION** in this chapter and **COMPOUND NOUN AND ADJECTIVE FORMS** in Chapter 2.

Example: self-taught writer; 100-foot path;
one-third; secretary-treasurer; vice-president;
quasi-public corporation; 4- by 6-inch cards;
anti-American; 1-800-556-1232; well-organized manuscript

PARENTHESES ( )

Used to enclose incidental comments and figures or letters in lists run into the text. No space between parentheses and enclosed material.
Example: The article supported his theory (see page 9). The meeting is on Friday, March 11 (?). We need (1) writers, (2) copyeditors, and (3) proofreaders.

PERIOD (.)

Used as decimals after numbers and letters in a list, after certain abbreviations, and at the end of a sentence. See also ELLIPSIS. Two spaces after a sentence; no space in numbers and letters.
Example: 11.671; a. Frontmatter / b. Body / c. Backmatter; ibid.; It's hot today.

QUESTION MARK (?)

Used to end a direct question and to show doubt. Two spaces after a sentence; no space when enclosed in parentheses.
Example: Is your report finished? Shall we have lunch on Monday? Tuesday? Wednesday? He will prepare the tables (?), but a freelancer will do the artwork.

QUOTATION MARKS (" " ' ')

Used to enclose precise quotations; single marks, for quotations within a quotation; also used for titles of articles, unpublished material, essays, television shows, short poems, and short musical works. Do not enclose indented (extract) quotations, slang, general use of the words *yes* and *no,* or words following *so-called.* No space between the word quoted and quotation marks. Notice that in the American style of punctuation, periods and commas are placed *inside* the quotation marks. Semicolons and colons are placed *outside* the quotation marks. See also **USE OF ITALICS IN TYPED AND PRINTED MATERIAL** and **USE OF QUOTED MATERIAL** in Chapter 4.
Example: "I know," he said. The instructor asked us to look at the chapter "Punctuation." This is Roger "Billy" Davis. I read about the so-called disturbance. The answer is no. "Now," she said, "let us return to the poem 'Wanderlust' "; then she called upon one of the students to read the opening passage.

SEMICOLON (;)

Used to separate clauses that do not have a connecting conjunction and to separate items in a series that already has commas. No space between preceding word and semicolon.
Example: His report is due now; in fact, it's late. The promotional tour will include Phoenix, Arizona; Las Vegas, Nevada; and Salt Lake City, Utah. The officers are Bette Foster, president; James Cronin, vice-president; Edward Janeway, secretary; and Lois Kennedy, treasurer.

SLASH (ALSO, DIAGONAL; SOLIDUS; VIRGULE) (/)

Used in fractions, identification numbers, abbreviations, for *per,* in dates (instead of a hyphen) indicating a span of periods or calendar years, and between lines of poetry run

into the text. No space before or after a slash, except equal space on either side between lines of poetry.
Example: ½; 0170435/AR9; B/L; rev./min.; fiscal year 1986/87; as Sara Teasdale said: "I make the most of all that comes / And the least of all that goes."

RULES OF WORD DIVISION

PRONUNCIATION

Use pronunciation as a guide to word division.
Example: pre-sent (to give; to introduce); pres-ent (a gift; time)

SYLLABLES AND LETTERS

Do not divide one-syllable words or words with fewer than six letters.
Example: through (*not:* th-rough); passed (*not:* pas-sed or pass-ed); story (*not:* sto-ry)

Avoid dividing a word *before* a single syllable or before or after a single letter.
Example: prolifera-tion (*not:* prolifer-ation); abate-ment (*not:* a-batement); cafete-ria (*not:* cafeteri-a)

Do not divide a word unless three or more characters, including the hyphen or other punctuation, remain on the top line or are carried to the bottom line.
Example: de-activate (de-); break-up, (up,)

PREFIXES AND SUFFIXES

Do not divide prefixes and suffixes; divide a word before or after its prefix or suffix. Divide a suffix between a double consonant rather than within the suffix.

Example: anti-union (*not:* an-tiunion); permis-sible (*not:* permissi-ble)

When a consonant is doubled before an *-ing* ending, divide the word between the two consonants (*but:* words that already have a double consonant should be divided after the double letter).

Example: deter-ring (*not:* deterr-ing); mill-ing (*not:* mil-ling)

HYPHENATED COMPOUNDS

Divide hyphenated compound words only at the hyphen.

Example: mother-in-law (*not:* mo-ther-in-law); vice-chairperson (*not:* vice-chair-person)

DASHES

Keep a dash on the top line.

Example: spelling— / and word division (*not:* spelling / —and word division)

ABBREVIATIONS AND ACRONYMS

Do not divide contractions, organization abbreviations, and acronyms.

Example: SEATO (*not:* SEA-TO; wasn't (*not:* was-n't)

NAMES

Avoid dividing proper names (if necessary, divide only between first and last names).
Example: Lou / Preston (*not:* Lou Pres-ton); F. R. / Pomeroy (*not:* F. / R. Pomeroy)

NUMBERS

Avoid dividing figures (if necessary, divide only at the comma).
Example: 2,711,-806,953 (*not:* 2,71-1,806,953)

Avoid separating figures from abbreviations, days from years (if necessary, separate a date only between day and year), and other number-word groups.
Example: page 79 (*not:* page / 79); 35 km (*not:* 35 / km); October 23, / 1985 (*not:* October / 23, 1985)

Separate numbered or lettered lists only before the number or letter.
Example: (1) research, / (2) writing, and (3) editing (*not:* [1] research, [2] / writing, and [3] editing)

Do not separate addresses between numbers and words.
Example: 2500 North / Forest Drive (*not:* 2500 / North Forest Drive

NOTE: See also **CORRECT USE OF NUMBERS AND FRACTIONS** in this chapter and **COMPOUND NOUN AND ADJECTIVE FORMS** in Chapter 2.

RULES OF CAPITALIZATION

EDUCATION

Capitalize the full, official titles of schools and colleges and the names of departments and divisions.
Example: Washington University; the university; Department of Economics; economics department

Capitalize the names of classes and the official titles of courses and programs.
Example: Junior Class; a junior; History 101; a history course; Black Studies Program; the program

Capitalize initials representing degrees and the honors that are part of a name or title.
Example: Paul S. Farnsworth Fellowship; the fellowship; Mary Goldsmith, Ph.D.; a doctor of philosophy

GEOGRAPHY

Capitalize political divisions and major parts of the world, the divisions or major regions of continents and countries, and official topographical names.
Example: Far East; West Coast; Middle Atlantic states; Western world; the South (region); southern (direction, locality); Orient; oriental culture; West Africa; western Africa; Colorado River; Colorado and Rio Grande rivers

Capitalize popular and legendary names of regions and localities.
Example: Badlands (South Dakota); Bay Area (San Francisco); Deep South (U.S.); Foggy Bottom (Washington, D.C.)

GOVERNMENT AND POLITICS

Capitalize the official titles of acts, bills, plans, treaties, laws, amendments, and constitutions.
Example: Salisbury Act; the act; Marshall Plan; First Amendment (U.S. Constitution); the amendment; the Constitution (U.S.); Georgia Constitution; the constitution (Georgia)

Capitalize the names of political parties (but not the word *party*) and the official titles of governmental, administrative, legislative, and deliberative bodies.
Example: Communist party; Communists; communism; the party; the Right; right wing; the General Assembly (UN); the assembly; Des Moines Board of Education; the board of education; U.S. Department of Labor; Labor Department; the department; Parliament (British); parliamentary

Capitalize political divisions, units, and other designations when they follow a name or are an accepted part of it.
Example: Roman Empire; the empire; Indiana State; the state of Indiana; Yapavi County; the county of Yapavi; Tenth Ward; the ward; the Union (U.S.)

HISTORY

Capitalize the official names of important events, plans, documents, early historical and cultural periods, major geological periods, and cultural movements derived from proper names.
Example: Great Depression; World War I; Mayflower Compact; Dark Ages; space age; colonial period (U.S.); twentieth century; Platonism; humanism; Gothic

HOLIDAYS, FESTIVALS, SEASONS, DAYS, AND TIME

Capitalize the names of religious seasons, religious and secular holidays, calendar months and days of the week, and abbreviations of time zones.
Example: Good Friday; New Year's Day; Veterans Day; election day; December; Thursday; summer solstice; EDT (eastern daylight time)

JUDICIARY

Capitalize the official titles of courts, judicial titles when they precede a proper name, and all important words in legal cases.
Example: U.S. Supreme Court, the Court (U.S. Supreme); Arizona Supreme Court; the supreme court (Arizona); American Bar Association; the bar; Justice Renquist; the justice; *Whitestone* v. *City of Los Angeles;* the *Whitestone* case

LISTS AND OUTLINES

Capitalize the first word of each item in a list or outline.
Example: I. Text content
        A. Body
          1. Introduction
          2. Chapters and appendixes

MILITARY

Capitalize military titles preceding a proper name and the full names and titles of military groups, wars and battles, craft and vessels, and awards and citations.
Example: Ruth Block, captain; Capt. (or Captain) Ruth

Block; the captain; Allied forces; National Guard; the guard; U.S. Coast Guard; the Coast Guard; Royal Air Force; British air force; U.S. Navy; the navy; Pacific Fleet; the fleet; Vietnam War; the war; SS *Enterprise;* ICBM; Medal of Honor; Henry Root, Admiral of the Fleet. (Admiral of the Fleet and General of the Army are always capitalized before and after a name to avoid ambiguity.)

PROPER NOUNS

Capitalize the names of particular persons, places, and things, including peoples, races, tribes (unless the description is based only on color, race, or local custom or is a noun, adjective, or verb derived from the capitalized description); epithets; fictitious names; trade names; and words that are personified. *Example:* Ronald Reagan; North America; Orientals; blacks; Don Quixote; quixotic; Babe Ruth; John Doe; Mother Nature; the Capitol (U.S. building); Romans; roman numerals; Coca-Cola

RELIGION

Capitalize names for the Bible and its books and divisions; other sacred religious works; references to the Deity in formal or religious writing; special events, rites, and services; and official names of specific churches. *Example:* Bible; biblical; Chronicles; the Scriptures; the Gospels; the gospel truth; Talmud; talmudic; Greek gods; Original Sin; the Mass (the eucharistic sacrament); high mass (an individual celebration); bar mitzvah; First Lutheran Church of Milwaukee; Lutheran church

SCIENTIFIC TERMS

Capitalize names of plants and animals above the species level (except general descriptive terms), geological eras, planets and satellites (but not meteorological phenomena), and chemical symbols.

Example: *Homo* (genus); *Homo sapiens* (genus + species); succulents; Pliocene epoch; Mars; Big Dipper; aurora borealis; H_2O

TITLES OF PERSONS

Capitalize titles when they precede a person's name (except for titles that are job descriptions, such as programmer).

Example: Vice-President Bush; George Bush, vice-president of the United States; the Reverend Edwards; the rector; postal clerk Roy Miller; the Queen Mother; the queen of England; Her Majesty; David Yorktowne, first earl of Stafford; the earl of Stafford; the physician Edna Prentiss; Dr. Edna Prentiss

TITLES OF WORKS

Capitalize all important words, including verbs, in titles of written works, musical compositions, paintings and sculptures, television and radio programs, motion pictures, and mottoes and notices.

Example: *Writer's Almanac and Fact Book* (book); *Newsweek* (magazine); "Radiation at Test Sites" (dissertation); "Dallas" (television show); the *Emperor* Concerto, Piano Concerto no. 5 (musical composition); *The Thinker* (sculpture); *The Old Mill* (painting); *The Divine Comedy* (long poem); No Smoking (notice)

2. ELEMENTS OF GRAMMAR

From the day we learn to speak, the elements of grammar are a part of our daily lives; from the day we learn to write, they are a tool that we unconsciously use to translate our facts, figures, and ideas into coherent and meaningful messages that will elicit some desired response from readers. Incorrect grammar can lead others to question our intelligence and doubt our competence. It can weaken or even destroy the effectiveness of our messages. Few of us can afford to risk the implications of grammatical weakness in our work, and no one with a healthy sense of pride would want to do so.

PARTS OF SPEECH AND GRAMMATICAL TERMS

Parts of Speech

ADJECTIVE

Modifies a noun or pronoun.
Example: a *strong* wind

ADVERB

Modifies a verb, an adjective, or another adverb.
Example: She worked *rapidly*.

CONJUNCTION

Connects other words.
Example: he *and* she

INTERJECTION

Expresses a strong or sudden feeling.
Example: Oh!

NOUN

Name of a person, place, thing, action, idea, or quality.
Example: *Wilson Company* (proper noun); a *company* (common noun)

PREPOSITION

Shows the relation between its object and another word.
Example: of; to

PRONOUN

Used in place of a noun.
Example: it; those

VERB

Denotes action or state of being.
Example: is; bring

Grammatical Terms

ACTIVE VOICE

Indicates that the subject of a sentence is providing the action. See also PASSIVE VOICE.
Example: I *wrote* the report.

ANTECEDENT

Noun or pronoun to which another pronoun refers.
Example: Bill (noun) finished his (pronoun) manuscript.

APPOSITIVE

Identifies or explains another word(s).
Example: Madeline Stowe, *editor* suggested further revision.

ARTICLE

Adjectives *a* and *an* (indefinite articles) and *the* (definite article).
Example: the typewriter

AUXILIARY VERB

Helps another verb form or verb phrase.
Example: The professor *is* lecturing.

CASE

Property of a noun or pronoun showing its relation to other words. *Nominative case:* noun or pronoun is used as the subject of a sentence; *objective case:* is used as the object of a verb or preposition; *possessive case:* is used to show ownership. See **BASIC FORMS OF PRONOUNS** in this chapter.
Example: She is here (nominative). The publisher returned the manuscript to Jane and *me* (objective). *My* work is finished (possessive).

COLLECTIVE NOUN

Name of a group or collection of objects.
Example: team; family

COMPARATIVE DEGREE

Used when comparing two persons or things. See also SUPERLATIVE DEGREE.
Example: Our proposal is *longer* than theirs.

COMPLEMENT

Completes the meaning of a verb.
Example: The supervisor dictated the *letter*.

COMPOUND PREDICATE

Two or more connected verbs or verb phrases.
Example: He *wrote* and *mailed* the article.

COMPOUND SENTENCE

Has two or more independent clauses.
Example: (1) The computer malfunctioned, but (2) the service department repaired it.

COMPOUND SUBJECT

Two or more words joined by *and, or, nor.*
Example: The *editor* and his *assistant* left early.

COORDINATE CONJUNCTION

Connects words, phrases, and clauses of equal importance.
Example: I wrote *and* he edited.

DANGLING MODIFIER

Does not refer to another word or does not modify any other word. See also MISPLACED MODIFIER.
Example: After hearing (dangling) from my agent, the clause was deleted. (*Better: After hearing* from my agent, *we* deleted the clause.)

DEPENDENT (SUBORDINATE) CLAUSE

Group of words in a sentence with a subject and predicate that alone does not express a complete thought.
Example: The woman *who was introduced first* is from the government.

DIRECT OBJECT

Noun or noun equivalent that receives a verb's action; answers the question *what* or *whom* after the verb.
Example: She answered (what?) the *phone*.

EXPLETIVE

Introductory word such as *it* or *there* that fills the position of the subject when the actual subject comes after the verb.
Example: There are two librarians on duty. (*Better:* Two librarians are on duty.)

FUTURE PERFECT TENSE

Denotes action to be completed at a definite future time.
Example: I *will have finished* the article by the time you need it.

FUTURE TENSE

Denotes future time.
Example: I *will attend* the conference next month.

GERUND

Verb form ending in *-ing* used as a noun; may be a subject, a direct object, an object of a preposition, a subjective complement, or an appositive.
Example: Running is a popular activity.

IMPERATIVE MOOD

Expresses a command or request; always present tense, second person.
Example: *Close* the door.

INDICATIVE MOOD

Used to say something or ask something.
Example: The president greeted the delegates (statement).

INDIRECT OBJECT

Noun or noun equivalent usually indicating to whom or for whom something is done; occurs before the direct object.
Example: The writer sent the *publisher* (indirect object) a letter (direct object).

INFINITIVE

Verb form used as a noun, an objective, or an adverb, usually preceded by *to*.
Example: She wanted *to see* the play.

INTRANSITIVE VERB

One that has no object. See also TRANSITIVE VERB.
Example: The time *passed* quickly.

LINKING VERB

Links a subject with another word that explains or describes it.
Example: The politician *is* an author.

MISPLACED MODIFIER

One positioned in a sentence so it appears to modify the wrong word. See also DANGLING MODIFIER.
Example: They *only* (misplaced) toured the archives.
(*Better:* They toured *only* the archives.)

MODIFIER

Word(s) that restricts or qualifies the meaning of another word.
Example: a *blue* sky

MOOD

Expresses the attitude of the speaker or writer (statement; question; wish; expression of possibility or doubt; command). See IMPERATIVE MOOD, INDICATIVE MOOD, and SUBJUNCTIVE MOOD.

NOMINATIVE CASE

Indicates the case of a subject or a predicate noun.
Example: Our *boss* (subject) is a former *astronaut* (predicate nominative).

NONRESTRICTIVE CLAUSE

Subordinate clause that is nonessential to the meaning of the sentence; usually set off with commas.
Example: The book, *which was just released*, is hard to comprehend.

OBJECTIVE CASE

Indicates the case of a direct object, an indirect object, or the object of a preposition.
Example: They gave *us* (indirect object of *gave*) the *money* (direct object of *gave*) to deposit in the *bank* (object of *in*).

PARTICIPLE

Verb form used as an adjective or predicate adjective.
Example: The *increasing* sales are encouraging.

PASSIVE VOICE

Indicates that the subject of a sentence is receiving the action (is being acted upon). See also ACTIVE VOICE.
Example: The instructions *were written* by me.

PAST PERFECT TENSE

Denotes action completed at some definite time in the past.
Example: I *had started* to write when the telephone rang.

PAST TENSE

Denotes past time.
Example: I *began* to type.

PERSON

Indicates who is speaking: *first person* (the one speaking); *second person* (the one being spoken to); *third person* (the

person or thing being spoken about). See **BASIC FORMS OF PRONOUNS** in this chapter.
Example: I edit the newsletter (first person). *You* edit the newsletter (second person). *They* edit the newsletter (third person).

POSSESSIVE CASE

Shows possession.
Example: the *woman's* car; *my* car

PREDICATE

Part of a sentence containing the verb and other words that make a statement about the subject.
Example: My friend Carl *is a designer*.

PREDICATE ADJECTIVE

Follows a linking verb and modifies the subject.
Example: The advice is *useful*.

PRESENT PERFECT TENSE

Denotes action completed at the time of speaking or writing (that also may be continuing into the present).
Example: He *has delivered* the flowers.

PRESENT TENSE

Denotes action occurring now.
Example: I *see* the results.

RELATIVE ADJECTIVE

Relative pronoun (for example, *whose*) used as an adjective.
Example: She is the attorney *whose* case was overturned.

RELATIVE ADVERB

Adverb (for example, *where, when, why*) referring to an antecedent in the main clause and modifying a word in the subordinate clause.
Example: I scheduled my writing for a time *when* I was alone.

RELATIVE PRONOUN

Pronoun (for example, *who/whom, which/that*) that takes the place of a noun and joins a dependent clause to a main clause. See **BASIC FORMS OF PRONOUNS** in this chapter.
Example: He is the one *who* is most likely to succeed.

RESTRICTIVE CLAUSE

Clause essential to the sentence's meaning.
Example: The office *that has the computer* will be enlarged.

SUBJECT

Word or group of words in a sentence about which a statement is made.
Example: The work is easy.

SUBJUNCTIVE MOOD

Used to express beliefs, doubts, wishes, uncertainty, and contrary-to-fact conditions.
Example: If I *were* younger, I *would join* the Peace Corps.

SUBORDINATE CONJUNCTION

Words such as *since, so that,* and *although* used to link subordinate and main clauses.
Example: I came today *because* I wanted to see you before you left.

SUPERLATIVE DEGREE

Used to compare more than two persons or things. See also COMPARATIVE DEGREE.
Example: This trip is the *longest* I've ever taken.

TENSE

Change in a verb's form to distinguish time. See PRESENT TENSE, PRESENT PERFECT TENSE, FUTURE TENSE, FUTURE PERFECT TENSE, PAST TENSE, and PAST PERFECT TENSE.

TRANSITIVE VERB

Expresses action or state of being and has a direct object. See also INTRASITIVE VERB.
Example: I *reviewed* (what?) your policy guidelines.

VERBAL

Verb form used as another part of speech. See GERUND, INFINITIVE, and PARTICIPLE.

VOICE

Indicates whether a subject is doing the acting or is receiving the action (being acted upon). See ACTIVE VOICE and PASSIVE VOICE.

BASIC FORMS OF PRONOUNS

Pronoun	*Subjective/Objective/ Possessive*
Personal	
First-person singular	I/me/my, mine
First-person plural	we/us/our, ours
Second-person singular and plural	you/you/your, yours
Third-person singular	he, she, it/him, her, it/his, her, hers, its
Third-person plural	they/them/their, theirs
Relative	who, that, which/whom, that, which/whose, of which
Interrogative	who, which, what/whom, which, what/whose, of which

Other Pronouns

Reflexive/intensive (myself, yourself, himself, herself, itself, oneself, ourselves, yourselves, themselves)

Demonstrative (this, these, that, those)

Indefinite (all, another, any, anybody, anyone, anything, both, each, each one, either, everybody, everyone, everything, few, many, most, much, neither, nobody, none, no one, nothing, one, other, several, some, somebody, someone, something, such)

Reciprocal (each other, one another)

Numeral (one, two, three . . . first, second, third . . .)

COMMON ENGLISH PREPOSITIONS

aboard	beside(s)	like	saving
about	between	mid	since
above	betwixt	midst	through
across	beyond	near	throughout
after	but	notwith- standing	till
against	by	of	to
along	concerning	off	touching
amid(st)	considering	on	toward(s)
among(st)	down	out	under
around	during	outside	underneath
aslant	ere	over	until
at	except	past	unto
athwart	excepting	pending	up
barring	for	per	upon
before	from	regarding	via
behind	in	respecting	with
below	inside	round	within
beneath	into	save	without

NOTE: Many prepositions are also used as other parts of speech. *Near,* for example, is also used as an adverb, an adjective, and a verb.

COMMON CONJUNCTIONS

also	if	since	whereas
although	lest	so	whereby
and	neither	still	wherefore
as	nevertheless	than	wherein
because	nor	that	whereof
both	notwith-standing	then	whereupon
but	only	therefore	wherever
either	or	though	whether
except	provided	unless	while
for	save	what	without
however	seeing	when	yet

CONJUGATION OF A REGULAR VERB

Tense	Indicative Mood (Active Voice)
Present	I *stop,* he *stops,* we *stop,* you *stop,* they *stop*
Present perfect	I *have stopped,* he *has stopped,* we *have stopped,* you *have stopped,* they *have stopped*
Past	I *stopped,* he *stopped,* we *stopped,* you *stopped,* they *stopped*

Tense	Indicative Mood (Active Voice)
Past perfect	I *had stopped*, he *had stopped*, we *had stopped*, you *had stopped*, they *had stopped*
Future Declarative	I *shall stop*, he *will stop*, we *shall stop*, you *will stop*, they *will stop*
Purposive	I *will stop*, he *shall stop*, we *will stop*, you *shall stop*, they *shall stop*
Future perfect Declarative	I *shall have stopped*, he *will have stopped*, we *shall have stopped*, you *will have stopped*, they *will have stopped*
Purposive	I *will have stopped*, he *shall have stopped*, we *will have stopped*, you *shall have stopped*, they *shall have stopped*

Subjunctive Mood (Active Voice)

Present	If: I *stop*, he *stop*, we *stop*, you *stop*, they *stop*
Present perfect	If: I *have stopped*, he *has stopped*, we *have stopped*, you *have stopped*, they *have stopped*
Past	If: I *stopped*, he *stopped*, we *stopped*, you *stopped*, they *stopped*
Past Perfect	If: I *had stopped*, he *had stopped*, we *had stopped*, you *had stopped*, they *had stopped*

Imperative Mood (Active Voice)

Present	*Stop* (meaning: you stop!)

NOTE: The three principal parts of the regular verb *stop* are *stop* (present), *stopped* (past), and *stopped* (past participle). The past and past participle of regular verbs such as *stop*, *call*, *look*, and *push* are always formed by adding *d* or *ed* (*push, pushed, pushed*). See also **COMMON IRREGULAR VERBS** in this chapter.

COMMON IRREGULAR VERBS

Present	*Past*	*Past Participle*
abide	abode	abode
arise	arose	arisen
be	was	been
bear	bore	borne
beat	beat	beaten/beat
become	became	become
begin	began	begun
behold	beheld	beheld
bid	bide/bade	bidden
bind	bound	bound
bite	bit	bitten
bleed	bled	bled
blow	blew	blown
break	broke	broken
breed	bred	bred
bring	brought	brought
build	built	built
burst	burst	burst
buy	bought	bought
cast	cast	cast
catch	caught	caught
choose	chose	chosen
cleave	cleft/clove/cleaved	cleft/cloven

Present	*Past*	*Past Participle*
cling	clung	clung
come	came	come
cost	cost	cost
creep	crept	crept
cut	cut	cut
deal	dealt	dealt
do	did	done
draw	drew	drawn
drink	drank	drunk
drive	drove	driven
eat	ate	eaten
fall	fell	fallen
feed	fed	fed
feel	felt	felt
fight	fought	fought
find	found	found
flee	fled	fled
fling	flung	flung
fly	flew	flown
forbid	forbade	forbidden
forget	forgot	forgotten
forsake	forsook	forsaken
freeze	froze	frozen
get	got	got/gotten
give	gave	given
go	went	gone
grind	ground	ground
grow	grew	grown
have	had	had
hide	hid	hidden
hit	hit	hit
hold	held	held
hurt	hurt	hurt
keep	kept	kept
know	knew	known

Present	Past	Past Participle
lay	laid	laid
lead	led	led
leave	left	left
lend	lent	lent
let	let	let
lie (recline)	lay	lain
lose	lost	lost
make	made	made
mean	meant	meant
meet	met	met
pay	paid	paid
put	put	put
read	read	read
rid	rid	rid
ride	rode	ridden
rise	rose	risen
run	ran	run
say	said	said
see	saw	seen
seek	sought	sought
sell	sold	sold
send	sent	sent
set	set	set
shake	shook	shaken
shed	shed	shed
shoot	shot	shot
shrink	shrank/shrunk	shrunk/shrunken
shut	shut	shut
sing	sang	sung
sink	sank/sunk	sunk
sit	sat	sat
slide	slid	slid
sling	slung	slung
speak	spoke	spoken
speed	sped	sped

Present	Past	Past Participle
spend	spent	spent
split	split	split
spread	spread	spread
spring	sprang/sprung	sprung
stand	stood	stood
steal	stole	stolen
stick	stuck	stuck
sting	stung	stung
strike	struck	struck/stricken
string	strung	strung
strive	strove	striven
swear	swore	sworn
sweep	swept	swept
swim	swam	swum
swing	swung	swung
take	took	taken
teach	taught	taught
tear	tore	torn
tell	told	told
think	thought	thought
throw	threw	thrown
thrust	thrust	thrust
tread	trod	trodden
wear	wore	worn
weep	wept	wept
win	won	won
wind	wound	wound
wring	wrung	wrung
write	wrote	written

NOTE: See also **CONJUGATION OF A REGULAR VERB** in this chapter.

VERB TENSES

PRESENT

Indicates action taking place now or habitual action or is used to express an idea generally accepted as true; *simple present* uses no auxiliary verb; *progressive present* is a combination of the present tense of *to be* and the present participle of the main verb.

Example: He *works* hard (simple present). He *is working* today (progressive present).

PRESENT PERFECT

Indicates action completed at the time of writing or speaking or continuing into the present; formed by combining *have* or *has* with the past participle of the main verb.

Example: He *has worked* in Detroit for two years.

PAST

Indicates action completed in the past.

Example: I *worked* at home today.

PAST PERFECT

Indicates action completed before a definite time in the past; formed by combining *had* with the past participle of the main verb.

Example: The salesperson *had started* the presentation by the time I arrived.

FUTURE

Indicates action that will take place in the future; formed by combining *will* or *shall* with the main verb.
Example: I *will arrive* on Sunday.

FUTURE PERFECT

Indicates action that will be completed at a definite time in the future; formed by combining *shall have* or *will have* with the past participle of the main verb.
Example: They *will have started* on their trip before noon.

NOTE: See also **CONJUGATION OF A REGULAR VERB** in this chapter.

POSITIVE, COMPARATIVE, AND SUPERLATIVE ADJECTIVE FORMS

POSITIVE

Basic form of an adjective used for simple description of a person or object.
Example: He seems *old* for his years.

COMPARATIVE

Form of adjective used to compare two persons or things, indicated by adding *-er* to the basic adjective or by placing the word *more* before it.

Example: His office was *larger* than I expected. The job is *more exciting* today than it was a year ago.

SUPERLATIVE

Form of adjective used to indicate that among more than two persons or things, one of them possesses the greatest degree of some quality; formed by adding *-est* to the basic adjective or by placing the word *most* before it.
Example: The hotel is the *largest* building on the block. The subject of mathematics is the *most difficult* for me.

NOTE: Irregular adjectives do not form comparative and superlative degrees by adding *-er* or *-est* or by placing *more* or *most* before the basic adjective. No standard pattern is used. For example: many/more/most; good, well/better/best; little/less/least; bad/worse/worst.

COMPOUND NOUN AND ADJECTIVE FORMS

Compound Nouns

OPEN

Nouns with two or more closely associated words that form a single concept but are written separately without a hyphen.
Example: attorney general (a single office), quasi corporation (as a noun; see also **Compound Adjectives, HYPHENATED**), decision maker, problem solving, father figure (expressions of relationship), master artist (*but:* masterpiece)

HYPHENATED

Nouns with two or more closely associated words or words of equal importance joined by hyphens.
Example: writer-editor (equal importance),
stick-in-the-mud, great-grandmother, ex-senator,
vice-consul, president-elect, father-in-law,
self-consciousness, one-half, five twenty-sevenths, 4-1 (as a ratio, using hyphen instead of colon), T-square (single letter for first word), crow's-nest (apostrophe in first word)

CLOSED

Nouns with two or more words or elements so closely associated that they are written as a single word.
Example: textbook (*but:* reference book),
toothache, grandson, bookkeeping (*but:* record keeping), clearinghouse

Compound Adjectives

OPEN

Adjectives with two or more parts that together modify a noun or pronoun but are written separately without a hyphen.
Example: She was *well informed* (most *predicate* adjectives), *social security* office (most well-established adjectives), a very *well known* book (a compound preceding a noun that has a modifier such as *very*), *South American* continent (most proper names), *highly efficient* machine (*-ly* adverb-adjective combinations), *very interesting* movie (adverb-adjective combinations). The salary increase *was* much *needed* (adverb-participle combinations with participle part of verb), *bluish* gray eyes (when first color modifies second), *sulfuric acid* solution (most chemical terms)

HYPHENATED

Adjectives with two or more parts that together modify a noun or pronoun and are joined by hyphens.

Example: *high-level* official (most adjectives *before* the nouns they modify), *450-mile* trip (number-noun combinations *before* the nouns they modify), *devil-may-care* attitude (coined phrases), *self-appointed* judge, *quasi-independent* corporation (as an adjective; see also **Compound Nouns, OPEN**), *all-inclusive* theory, *cross-ventilated* room, *up-to-date* list, *tax-exempt* (some adjectives *before* or *after* a noun), *Canada-United States* cooperation (proper names of equal weight)

CLOSED

Adjectives with two or more parts that together modify a noun or pronoun and are written as a single word.

Example: bird*like* appetite (*but:* hill-*like* terrain), nation*wide* vote, three*fold* increase, *counter*productive efforts, *multi*national force

NOTE: Since many exceptions to the general style described here occur in both noun and adjective forms, refer to a dictionary or modern style book when in doubt. See also **RULES OF WORD DIVISION** and **SPELLING GUIDELINES** in Chapter 1.

CLASSIFICATION OF PHRASES

NOUN PHRASE

A noun and associated words that function as a unit.

Example: *The woman with the black briefcase* is our guest speaker.

VERB PHRASE

A principal verb and one or more of the auxiliary verbs (*be, can, do, have, may, must, shall, will, ought,* and sometimes *let*).
Example: The plane *may have arrived.*

PREPOSITIONAL PHRASE

A preposition, its object, and any modifiers of the object; functions as an adjective or adverb.
Example: The package came *from the Research Institute.*

PARTICIPIAL PHRASE

A participle plus its object or complement and modifiers; functions as an adjective or adverb.
Example: Complaining loudly, the driver waited in the traffic.

GERUND PHRASE

A gerund plus its object or complement and modifiers; functions as a noun.
Example: Reading rapidly helps in my work.

INFINITIVE PHRASE

An infinitive with its subject and other accompanying words; functions as a noun, adjective, or adverb.
Example: To cheat is wrong.

CLASSIFICATION OF CLAUSES

INDEPENDENT CLAUSE

A subject and predicate that could stand alone as a sentence.
Example: They celebrated because their seminar was a huge success.

DEPENDENT CLAUSE

A subordinate adverbial, adjectival, or noun clause that could not stand alone as a sentence.
Example: The procedure, *which is well defined,* is to verify all figures before typing.

ADVERBIAL CLAUSE

Functions as an adverb and modifies a verb, adjective, other adverb, or an entire other clause.
Example: You may leave *when the letter is finished.*

ADJECTIVAL CLAUSE

Functions as an adjective and modifies a noun or pronoun.
Example: The editor *who works for Mr. Johnson* is in charge of mailing lists.

NOUN CLAUSE

Functions as a noun and is used as a subject, object of a verb, or object of a preposition.
Example: It's true *that retail sales are up.*

NOTE: Nonrestrictive adjective clauses are set off with commas (his book, *which has sold numerous copies,* describes the solar system). *Restrictive* clauses are *not* set off with commas (the book *that has a torn page* is mine).

MAJOR CLASSES OF SENTENCES

Structure

SIMPLE

One subject and one predicate.
Example: John and Mary (*subject*) will cosponsor the seminar (*predicate*).

COMPOUND

Two or more simple sentences.
Example: (1) The editor recommended that Chapter 4 be deleted, and (2) the author readily complied.

COMPLEX

One simple sentence combined with one or more dependent clauses.
Example: The person *who submitted the proposal* is likely to receive a promotion.

COMPOUND-COMPLEX

Two or more simple sentences combined with one or more dependent clauses.

Example: Althcugh quality control has been improved, (1) the product is still substandard, and (2) sales are still declining.

Meaning

DECLARATIVE

A statement.
Example: The meeting is scheduled for Friday.

IMPERATIVE

A command or request.
Example: Look in the files.

INTERROGATIVE

A question.
Example: Is the letter finished?

EXCLAMATORY

Strong feeling.
Example: That's not true!

3. CONTEMPORARY CORRESPONDENCE

Millions of dollars are generated every year by letter. Products, services, plans, ideas, and almost anything else you can name are sold by mail. Form letters as well as personal letters are designed to motivate people to take some action or to respond in some way; both business and social writers want recipients of their letters and memos to form a certain impression. Because tone, accuracy, neatness, style, and many other aspects of letter writing convey a distinct image of your sincerity, professionalism, and intelligence, well-developed letter-writing skill is a strong asset and a formidable tool you can use to reap lasting benefits.

BASIC LETTER FORMATS

Full-Block Letter Format

July 6, 1985

CONFIDENTIAL

Ms. Anne Greenlawn
Inland Printing Company
2020 Hudson Avenue
Jacksonville, FL 32206

Dear Ms. Greenlawn:

Subject: Full-Block Letter Format

If you want your letters to have a clean, modern look, the full-block format illustrated here would be a good choice.

Notice that the principal parts in this style are typed against the left margin. The body of the letter is single spaced, with a double space between paragraphs and between most basic parts of the letter.

The subject line is typed immediately after the salutation. If you used an attention line, it would be placed above the salutation.

Many writers like this letter format because it saves time. With all parts typed flush left, you don't have to pause to set up and use tabulator stops.

Sincerely,

Don Canoga
Editor

fm

Enc.

cc: Michael Romano

Block Letter Format

July 6, 1985

Our file 71AJ2

Trinity Industries
841 Phillips Road
Columbia, SC 29205

Attention: Henry Sutter III

Ladies and Gentlemen:

Have you considered a block letter format for your company? Unlike the full-block style, the block format does not show all parts positioned flush left. It therefore has a more traditional appearance, which you may prefer.

Notice that the dateline and the reference line are typed against the right margin, and the complimentary close and signature line are typed just to the right of the page center. All other elements, however, are typed flush left as they are in the full-block style.

Some writers like this format because it looks traditional, and yet some time is saved in setup since the paragraphs don't have to be indented.

Sincerely,

Don Canoga
Editor

mj

P.S. If you would like additional information about letter formats, please let me know. DC

Modified-Block Letter Format

July 6, 1985

Your ref. 811006F

Mr. Harold Aldridge
Investment Counsellors, Inc.
One King Avenue
Lynn, MA 01907

Dear Mr. Aldridge:

Subject: Modified-Block Letter Format

This letter is typed in a modified-block format. It differs from the block letter style in that paragraphs, the subject line, and the postscript are indented.

Notice that the dateline and reference line in this style, like the block format, are typed against the right margin, and the complimentary close and signature line are typed just to the right of the page center. But the indentation of major parts such as the paragraphs gives the letter even more of a traditional appearance than in the block style.

The trend is toward more modern letter styles such as the block letter and the simplified letter, but the traditional modified-block format is still preferred in many offices.

Sincerely,

Don Canoga
Editor

ls

Simplified Letter Format

July 6, 1985

Mrs. Jacob Goldberg
American Insurance Agency
3077 105th Street, N.E.
Seattle, WA 98125

SIMPLIFIED FORMAT

The simplified letter format, Mrs. Goldberg, is even easier
to use than the full-block style. It's a format that ap-
peals to many writers in modern offices.

Notice that this style does not use a salutation or complimentary close. The subject line is typed in all capitals
without the word "Subject," and the signature is also typed
in capital letters on one line. Everything is typed against
the left margin, as it is in the full-block style, so there are
no tabs to set up and use.

To avoid an impersonal tone, Mrs. Goldberg, since there
is no salutation, or complimentary close, this format
mentions the addressee's name in the opening and closing paragraphs.

DON CANOGA—EDITOR

fo

Official Letter Format

July 6, 1985

Dear Miss Pettis:

The official letter format illustrated here is used for personal and official letters. It looks particularly appealing on executive-size stationery.

Notice that this style, like the modified-block format, has indented paragraphs and shows the dateline typed flush right. The complimentary close and signature line are typed just to the right of the page center.

But this style differs from the others in that the inside address is placed against the left margin from two to five spaces below the final line of the signature. Any enclosure notation would then be given two spaces below the address. Identification initials are not typed on the original, but the dictator's name is typed in the signature line.

Sincerely yours,

Don Canoga
Editor

Miss Sonja Pettis
Hastings Business Services
P.O. Box 2624
Redding, CA 96099

BASIC MEMO FORMATS

Note Memo Format

M E M O from Don Canoga

The small note format, which is the simplest memo style,
is typically printed and bound in small note pads. This
type of note is used primarily for brief, informal (often
handwritten) messages to coworkers and business associates. A wide variety of memo and note pads is available in office supply and stationery stores; some companies
have a supply printed for each employee.

Standard Memo Format

To: Paul Eldridge   From: Don Canoga

Subject: Standard Memo Format   Date: July 6, 1985

It may be misleading to refer to a standard memo format, because memo styles range from preprinted multiple-
copy sets and speed-message pads to company-designed
letterheads. Unlike a brief memo note pad, this format
uses guide words, such as To, From, Subject, Date, Our Ref.
and Your Ref., positioned at the top of the page below
the printed letterhead address. Some styles have a line
for the signature at the bottom of the sheet, and other
styles divide the page into two parts; the sender writes
on one part, and the receiver replies on the other part.

The paragraphs in a standard memo resemble those in
an informal letter. Frequently, the paragraphs are typed
flush left as they are in full-block, block, and simplified
letters. The memo has no signature line; however, some
writers type or write their initials below the last line of
the body. Miscellaneous notations such as Enc. are
placed flush left two spaces below the last line or the writer's initials.

The memo, once common only in interoffice correspondence, is now also used for informal external correspondence such as informal notes to associates, brief
transmittal messages, and various purchase orders and
replies.

                        DC

mv

cc: Jill Ulster

PRINCIPAL PARTS OF LETTERS

ATTENTION LINE

An attention line is used in letters addressed to a firm to insure that if the person named in the attention line is absent, someone else will open the letter. Type this line two spaces below the inside address at the left margin. See **BASIC LETTER FORMATS, Block Letter Format,** in this chapter. On the envelope, type the attention line left of the address block on any line above the second line from the bottom of the address or immediately beneath the company name within the address block.

BODY

The message portion of a letter usually begins after the salutation or subject line. In the simplified format, it begins after the inside address or subject line. See **BASIC LETTER FORMATS** in this chapter. Type the paragraphs single-spaced, with a line space between them, and indent them or type them flush left, depending on the letter format being used.

CARBON-COPY NOTATION

A *regular* carbon-copy notation, which is typed on the original and on all copies, is used to specify who will receive copies of the letter. See **BASIC LETTER FORMATS, Full-Block Letter Format,** in this chapter. A *blind*-copy notation (*bcc: Jeremy Holt*), which is typed in the upper left corner of a letter *only* on that particular carbon copy and on your file copy, is used when you do not want the addressee to know that you are sending a copy of the letter elsewhere.

COMPLIMENTARY CLOSE

In all styles except the simplified format, which omits the closing, the complimentary close is typed two spaces below the last line of the last paragraph. See **BASIC LETTER FORMATS** in this chapter for the proper position. Use a personal, informal closing for general business and social letters (*Sincerely, Cordially, Regards, Best regards, Best wishes*). Use formal closings such as *Yours very truly* and *Respectfully* only in legal and official correspondence. (The closing phrase *I remain* is no longer used in contemporary correspondence.) See **FORMAL AND INFORMAL COMPLIMENTARY CLOSES** in this chapter.

CONTINUATION PAGE

Any page after the first page of a letter is a continuation page. Do not use the word *continued* or the abbreviation *cont.* at the bottom of the first page. Type a heading on the continuation page consisting of the addressee's name, the date, and the page number. The heading may be typed across the top of the page on one line or stacked, flush left.

Example: Donna Parsons
June 17, 1985
page three

DATELINE

Type the date at the top of the page two or more spaces beneath the letterhead information. See **BASIC LETTER FORMATS** in this chapter. The traditional business and social style is *November 7, 1985*. The military and some other organizations use the style *7 November 1985*.

ENCLOSURE NOTATION

An enclosure notation is typed at the bottom of the letter two lines beneath the identification line. See **BASIC LETTER FORMATS, Full-Block Letter Format,** in this chapter. Various styles are acceptable.

Example: Enclosure
Enc.
Encs. 3
Enclosures: Contract; Affidavit
Under separate cover: Catalog

IDENTIFICATION LINE

Initials in an identification line indicate who dictated and typed the letter. The identification line is usually typed two spaces below the signature, flush left. See **BASIC LETTER FORMATS** in this chapter. You may omit the initials on the original, but they should appear on each file copy. You may also omit the dictator's initials when his or her name appears in the signature line. When all initials are given, the initials of the person signing the letter appear first, followed by those of the dictator and then those of the typist (AM:CU:gf). use all capital letters for the dictator and the signer.

INSIDE ADDRESS

Type the inside address flush left. See **BASIC LETTER FORMATS** in this chapter. When the addressee's name is unknown, use a job title such as *Regional Director* if known. When the addressee's name is known, omit the job title if it would make the address run beyond four lines. Use the same data on the envelope. (For automated sorting, the U.S. Postal Service asks that the envelope address be typed in all capitals, single-spaced, in block form, at least one inch from the left of and five-eighths inch from the bottom of the envelope.) Use two-letter postal abbreviations for states and five- or nine-digit zip codes on the inside address as well as on the envelope address. See also **CONTEMPORARY FORMS OF ADDRESS** in this chapter.

MAIL NOTATION

Type a notation such as *Special Delivery* above the inside address only on carbon copies. On the envelope, type the notation two to four spaces beneath the postage.

PERSONAL OR CONFIDENTIAL NOTATION

Type a notation such as *Personal* or *Confidential*, under-lined beneath the dateline or in all capitals, against the left margin, two to four spaces above the inside address. On the envelope, type the notation in all capitals to the left of and two lines above the address block.

POSTSCRIPT

A postscript is used for comments unrelated to the message of the letter, not for remarks that you neglected to include in the body of the letter. Type it beneath the last notation and place the sender's initials immediately after the postscript message. See **BASIC LETTER FORMATS, Block Letter Format,** in this chapter.

REFERENCE LINE

When a reference line such as *Please refer to* or *In reply, please refer to* is not printed on the letterhead, type it two spaces beneath the dateline. See **BASIC LETTER FOR-MATS, Block Letter Format** and **Modified-Block Letter Format,** in this chapter.

SALUTATION

Except in the simplified style, which omits the salutation, a greeting is typed two spaces below the inside address, flush left. See **BASIC LETTER FORMATS** in this chapter. The trend is toward informal greetings in general business and social letters (*Dear Paula* or *Dear Ms. Snow*). Use formal greetings such as *Sir* or *My dear Mr. Jacobs* only in official correspondence. See **CORRECT LETTER SALUTATIONS** in this chapter.

SIGNATURE

Type the signature line four spaces below the complimentary close (five spaces below the last line of the body in the simplified letter style). See **BASIC LETTER FORMATS** in this chapter. Women may put *Miss* or *Mrs.* in parentheses before their names to signal that they want to be addressed as such; otherwise, readers will assume that they prefer to be addressed as *Ms.* (Do *not* type *Ms.* or *Mr.* before a signature unless necessary to show that a name such as *Leslie* is male or female.) Professional persons may add initials such as *M.D.* after their names. A company name is usually typed in all capitals two lines beneath the complimentary close. The name of the person signing the letter is then typed four lines beneath the company name. See **CORRECT SIGNATURE LINES** in this chapter.

SUBJECT LINE

Type the subject line two spaces below the salutation (three spaces beneath the inside address in the simplified letter style). Attorneys often use the words *In re* or *Re* instead

of *Subject* and place the line two spaces above the salutation. See **BASIC LETTER FORMATS** in this chapter. In general business and social letters, the trend is away from underscoring and the use of all capitals.

PRINCIPAL PARTS OF MEMOS

HEADING

Memo stationery often has headings printed at the top of the page beneath the letterhead address: *Date, To, From, Subject*. The typist fills in the appropriate information after each guide word. Major words in the subject line are capitalized. See **BASIC MEMO FORMATS** in this chapter.

BODY

The body of a memo is typed like the body of a letter, with paragraphs that may or may not be indented (memo paragraphs are frequently typed flush left). See **BASIC MEMO FORMATS** in this chapter. Since a memo has no salutation, the first paragraph begins two or more spaces after the last row of guide words.

NOTATIONS

Type miscellaneous notations such as the enclosure line in the same position as in a traditional letter. See **BASIC MEMO FORMATS** in this chapter.

ENVELOPE

Although the memo has no inside address, the envelope should be addressed the same as it would be for a letter. See the various references to envelope addressing in **PRINCIPAL PARTS OF LETTERS** in this chapter.

CORRECT LETTER SALUTATIONS

CAPITALIZATION

Capitalize the first word in a salutation and the person's name and title.
Example: Dear Mrs. Creston; Right Reverend Monsignor; Your Excellency; Dear Rabbi Goldberg

TITLES

Abbreviate the personal titles *Mr., Mrs., Messrs.,* and the professional title *Dr.*
Example: Dear *Mr.* Fremont; Dear *Mrs.* McClure; Dear *Messrs.* Corto and El Camino; Dear *Dr.* Mahaska

Spell out religious, military, and professional titles such as *Father, Major,* and *Professor.*
Example: Dear *Sister* Margaret; Dear *Major* Spencer; Dear *Professor* Dauber

MEN AND WOMEN

In salutations to more than one woman, use individually preferred titles if known; otherwise, use *Mss.* (or *Mses.*), *Misses,* or *Mesdames.*

Example: Dear *Ms*. Dorr, *Miss* Cutter, and *Mrs*. Brookridge; Dear *Mrs*. Cone and *Mrs*. Wingate; Dear *Mesdames* Cone and Wingate; Dear *Ms*. Vigo and *Ms*. Terrell; Dear *Mss*. Vigo and Terrell

In salutations to more than one man, use *Mr*. with each name or *Messrs*. or *Gentlemen*.
Example: Dear *Mr*. Moore and *Mr*. Idell; Dear *Messrs*. Moore and Idell; *Gentlemen*

In salutations to men and women, each addressed by name, use *Mr*. and *Ms*. or the woman's preferred title.
Example: Dear *Mr*. Myer and *Ms*. Egan; Dear *Mr*. Dupree and *Mrs*. Eldena

NAME AND GENDER UNKNOWN

Use the person's full name when the gender of the addressee is unknown.
Example: Dear R. F. Drummond; Dear Leslie Chatsworth.

Use *Sir* and *Madam* when name or name and gender are unknown.
Example: Dear *Sir;* Dear *Madam;* Dear *Madam or Sir;* Dear *Sir or Madam*

COMPANIES AND GROUPS

Use *Ladies* or *Mesdames* and *Gentlemen* or *Messrs*. when an organization is composed entirely of men or women; otherwise, designate both men and women in the salutation.
Example: Ladies; Gentlemen; Ladies and Gentlemen

In letters to groups of persons, use a collective term.
Example: Dear *Friends;* Dear *Members;* Dear *Employees*

FORMAL GREETINGS

Use formal greetings such as *My dear* only in official and formal correspondence.

Example: My dear Mrs. Reagan; *Right Reverend and dear Sir*

NOTE: See also **CONTEMPORARY FORMS OF ADDRESS** in this chapter.

FORMAL AND INFORMAL COMPLIMENTARY CLOSES

Formal	*Informal*
Respectfully	Sincerely
Respectfully yours	Sincerely yours
Yours truly	Cordially
Yours very truly	Cordially yours
Very truly yours	Regards
Very sincerely yours	Best regards
Very cordially yours	Warmest regards
	Best wishes

NOTE: Informal closings are used in most personal and business correspondence. Formal closings should be used only in legal, official, and other formal correspondence.

CONTEMPORARY FORMS OF ADDRESS

TITLES

A title precedes a name unless *Esq.* or initials such as *M.D.* follow the name. (The abbreviation *Esq.* is sometimes used in addressing prominent attorneys and other high-ranking officials who do not have other titles.) A title is used with initials only when the two are not synonymous (*not: Dr.* and *M.D.* together). But a religious order may be listed after a name even when a religious title such as *Father* is used.

Example: Ms. Elsie Seneca; *Mr.* A. J. Reaves II; *Professor* Sally Tazewell; Mary Talahi, *Esq.; The Honorable* Mary Talahi; *Dr.* Adam Solomon; Adam Solomon, *M.D.; Father* Lee Calhoun, *S.J.*

SCHOLASTIC DEGREES

Generally, avoid using degrees in an inside address. But if a professional person prefers that you use them, omit the title *Dr., Miss, Mrs., Ms.,* or *Mr.* before the name. (If necessary, you may use a descriptive title such as *Professor* or *Reverend* before a name with the person's degrees after it.) If someone has several degrees, list the one pertaining to the person's occupation first.

Example: John Church, *M.D.;* Dr. John Church; *The Reverend* Thomas Loftin, *D.D., Sc.D.*

GENDER AND NAME UNKNOWN

Omit titles such as *Mr.* and *Ms.* when the gender is unknown. Use a job title, if known, when a name is unavailable.
Example: Leslie Hodges; H. C. Foley; *Acting Mayor* of Des Moines; *Director of Research*

RETIRED OFFICIALS

Use *The Honorable* when a person has held an official title. Do not use political titles such as *Senator* and *President* after retirement, but do use titles of retired military officers. The title *Judge* may also be used after retirement.

Example: The Honorable Roberta Miller/*Dear Madam* or *Dear Ms.* Miller (former governor); *The Honorable* Jonathan Bernstein/*Sir* or *Dear Judge* Bernstein (retired judge); *Admiral* Edward Atmore, *U.S.N., Retired/Dear Admiral* Atmore

SINGLE WOMAN

Business, social-business, and informal social occasions: Use *Ms.*, unless you know that she prefers *Miss.*
Example: Ms. [or *Miss*] Alice Newton

Formal social occasions: Use *Miss.*
Example: Miss Alice Newton

MARRIED AND WIDOWED WOMAN

Business, social-business, and informal social occasions: Use *Ms.*, unless you know that she prefers *Mrs.* Use her first name and married last name, unless you know that professionally she uses her maiden name (with *Ms.* or *Miss*) or maiden and married names combined (with *Ms.* or *Mrs.*).
Example: Ms. [or *Mrs.*] Eleanore Berlin; *Ms.* [or *Miss*] Eleanore Hyatt; *Ms.* [or *Mrs.*] Eleanore Hyatt-Berlin

Formal social occasions: Use *Mrs.* with her husband's full name.
Example: Mrs. James Berlin

DIVORCED WOMAN

Business, social·business, and informal social occasions:
Use *Ms.* with her first name and married last name, unless
she has returned to her maiden name or uses her maiden and
married names combined. Use *Mrs.* with her married name or
Miss with her maiden name only if you know that she prefers
it.

Example: Ms. [or *Mrs.*] Rita Cortez; *Ms:* [or *Miss*] Rita
Bolivar; *Ms.* [or *Miss*] Rita Bolivar-Cortez; *Mrs.* Rita
Bolivar-Cortez

Formal social occasions: If she retains her married name,
use *Mrs.* with her maiden and married names combined. If
she prefers her maiden name only, use *Miss.* If she prefers
her first name and maiden and married names combined, use
Mrs.

Example: Mrs. Bolivar-Cortez; *Mrs.* Rita Cortez; *Miss* Rita
Bolivar; *Mrs.* Rita Bolivar-Cortez

PROFESSIONAL WOMAN

Use her professional title and her first and last (married)
names (or maiden or maiden-married name combination if
she prefers it).

Example: Dr. Anita Domingo; *Professor* Anita Largo;
Congresswoman Anita Largo-Domingo

HUSBAND AND WIFE

Use professional titles for both. If there is no title, use *Mr.* or
Mrs. When married women are addressed individually, follow the guidelines for married and widowed women.

Example: Mr. and *Mrs.* Roy Banks; *Dr.* and *Mrs.* Roy Banks; *Drs.* Julie and Roy Banks; *Dr.* Julie and *Mr.* Roy Banks; *Dr.* Julie Banks and *Mr.* Roy Banks

COMPANIES

Use single-sex designations for organizations consisting solely of either men or women; otherwise, refer to both. But do not use single-sex designations with impersonal organization names (*not: Messrs.* Campbell Manufacturing Company).
Example: Mesdames Holly and Rowe (all women); *Messrs.* Neches, Zurana, and Conrad (all men)

NOTE: See also **CORRECT LETTER SALUTATIONS** in this chapter.

CORRECT SIGNATURE LINES

COMPANY

Type the name in all capitals (as it appears on the letterhead) two spaces below the complimentary close, with the signer's name four spaces below the firm name.
Example: Sincerely yours,

SOFTWARE PUBLISHERS, INC.

Vincent Oakes

Vincent Oakes
Managing Editor

MAN

Type the name, without *Mr.*, exactly as the person signs it (type *Mr.* in parentheses before the name only when it is not clear whether the signer is a man or woman). Type any initials such as academic degrees after the name and put the job title on the next line.

Example:

Leslie Page

(Mr.) Leslie Page, CPA
General Accounting Manager

SINGLE WOMAN

Type *Miss* in parentheses before the name only if the signer prefers to include it. Do not use *Ms.* in the signature line unless it is not otherwise clear that the signer is a woman. You may type a short job title on the same line as the name.

Example:

Marge West

Marge West, Editor

Marge West

(Miss) Marge West, Editor

MARRIED OR WIDOWED WOMAN

Type *Mrs.* in parentheses before the name only if the signer prefers to include it. Do not use *Ms.* in the signature

line unless it is not otherwise clear that the signer is a woman.
Example:

Thelma Rose

Thelma Rose
Professor of History

Thelma Rose

(Mrs.) Thelma Rose
Professor of History

In social letters, type her husband's full name preceded by *Mrs.* in parentheses beneath the written signature.
Example:

Thelma Rose

(Mrs. Mark F. Rose)

DIVORCED WOMAN

Type *Miss* or *Mrs.* in parentheses before the name only if the signer prefers to include it.
Example:

Laura White

Laura White
Publicity Director

Laura White

(Mrs.) Laura White
Publicity Director

Use *Mrs.* only if she retains her married name or uses her maiden and married names combined.
Example:

Laura Boswick-White

(Mrs. Boswick-White)

Use *Miss* if she uses her maiden name. Do not use her former husband's first name in any instance and do not use *Ms.* in the signature line unless it is not otherwise clear that the signer is a woman.
Example:

Laura Boswick

(Miss) Laura Boswick

SECRETARY

If the secretary is the signer, follow the above rules for men and women. Do not use the employer's first name after *Secretary to Mr./Ms.* unless another person in the firm has the same last name.
Example:

Martin Siers

Martin Siers
Vice-President, Sales

Helena Goss

Helena Goss
Secretary to Mr. Siers

NOTE: A personal title such as *Miss* typed in parentheses before a name means that the writer wants to be addressed by that title. If no personal title is given in parentheses before a woman's name, the signer wants to be addressed as *Ms.* The initials *M.D.* after a name mean that the writer wants to be addressed as *Dr.* A professional title such as *Professor* or a military rank such as *Lieutenant, USAF* typed beneath a name means that the writer wants to be addressed by that title or rank.

MODEL LETTERS

Acknowledgment

Dear Ms. Webster:

Thanks very much for your June 19 proposal to expand the company library. Your preliminary suggestions are interesting, and I would like to discuss them with some of our departmental heads next week. I'll let you know by June 27 whether we have enough support to proceed with your plan.

I know everyone will appreciate the time and attention you gave to this project, Ms. Webster. Such contributions are always welcome and essential to growth and progress in our company.

Regards,

Adjustment

Dear Mr. Esmond:

We are sorry to learn that some of the Grade
10 binders in our August 19 shipment have a blemish
on their covers. Although such marks do occur in this
grade of binder, we understand that you may not have
known this, and we appreciate your concern.

Unfortunately, binders cannot be returned when
they have been embossed with a company name. However, we would like to offer you a 10 percent discount on
the entire shipment in the hope that this savings will
be helpful to you.

We greatly value your business, Mr. Esmond, and
will do our best to fill future orders to your satisfaction.

Sincerely,

Appreciation

Dear Elaine:

Many thanks for your help in the office during
my absence last week. Without your assistance in or-
ganizing and monitoring the monthly promotional mailing, we would surely have missed our deadline. But
thanks to you we made it—with one day to spare!

If ever I can reciprocate, Elaine, just let me know.

Best wishes,

Collection

Dear. Ms. Bledsoe:

Another thirty days have passed, and your payment of $191.98 is now sixty days past due.

Since we have not heard from you, we assume
that the balance shown in your records agrees with
ours. Won't you therefore send us your check immediately and protect your credit rating?

Your cooperation will be very much appreci-
ated, Ms. Bledsoe, Thank you.

Sincerely,

Congratulations

Dear Tanya:

I was delighted to learn about your promotion—
congratulations! You're well qualified for this important position, and I know you'll find your new duties
stimulating and challenging.

Best wishes for success, Tanya.

Cordially,

Follow-up

Dear Mr. Bradley:

You recently asked about the new A–Z Spell-
Checker, and I wanted to let you know that we now have
this software in stock. Would you like to stop by and see
it in action?

The enclosed brochure describes some of its features, such as detecting grammatical errors and other
common mistakes and checking your documents for misused words and phrases. It comes in two versions—with
or without independent dictionary expansion.

I hope you can come in soon—before our supply is exhausted—and see for yourself how much the

A–Z Spell-Checker can do. We're open from nine to six o'clock, Monday through Saturday. In the meantime, if you have any questions, feel free to phone me any time at 445-9900 or 446-1717.

Cordially,

Introduction

Dear Mrs. Odet:

It's a pleasure to introduce Joel Roger Finley to you as a possible candidate for an editorial position with your magazine.

Joel was previously a staff editor at Promotional Services in Washington, D.C. For the past year he has been freelancing in Phoenix and has written and edited several things for us: a brochure, an annual report, and a personnel handbook. In each case, we were pleased with his skill and care in producing an accurate document precisely tailored to our needs and interests. During each job, he was very cooperative and worked hard to meet our deadlines.

I'd appreciate any consideration you can give to him, and if I can provide any further information, Mrs. Odet, just let me know. Thanks very much.

Sincerely,

Invitation

Dear Dr. Canino:

Members of the Language and Communication Association have been very impressed with your theories on computer-mediated communication and would enjoy learning more about the process you advocate. We would like to invite you to speak on this subject at our

October 14, 1985, meeting at two o'clock in the conference hall of the Wayside Hotel, 1211 North Avenue, Fort
Smith, Arkansas. A twenty-minute address followed by
a ten-minute question and answer session would be ideal.

About one hundred persons—members and
nonmembers—are expected to attend. Most of them will
be instructors, writers, and editors who either teach
writing and communication or are in some way responsible for the production of written material. Many of
them, however, are using computer technology for the first
time or are merely contemplating its use. They would,
therefore, be most receptive to your theories as they apply to individuals in the learning stages.

In case you are able to be with us, I'm enclos-
ing a data form for you to complete; this will help us
publicize your appearance. Details concerning transpor-
tation and accommodations for speakers are included on
the enclosed Speaker's Information Form.

We do hope you can join us on October 14,
Dr. Canino. I'd appreciate having your reply by
August 30 so that we can complete our advance program
on schedule.

Sincerely,

Sympathy

Dear Tom:

Laura and I were deeply saddened by the death
of your wife, Karin. We both enjoyed visiting with her
at our many company events, and I know that everyone
will miss her very much.

Our heartfelt sympathy goes out to you and your
family. Do let me know if there is any way I can be of
help in the weeks ahead.

With sincerest sympathy,

Welcome

Dear Ben:

It's a pleasure to welcome you to our production staff. We have an exciting schedule of activity for the coming year, and I know you'll find numerous opportunities to use your many talents and skills.

The rest of our team are eager to work with you and will be glad to help you become acquainted with our procedures. I'll be looking forward to working with you too, Ben. Stop by my office any time you have questions and do let me know if I can help you in any way.

Best regards,

MODEL MEMOS

Announcement

Subject: Winter Carnival—December 9, 1985

The directors of Westview Distributors are pleased to announce that this year's Winter Carnival will be held on Saturday, December 9, 1985, from 6 until 10 p.m. in the company cafeteria and conference hall.

A delicious complimentary smorgasbord for employees and their guests will be available in the cafeteria from 6 until 9 p.m., with refreshments, music, and dancing in the conference hall throughout the evening. As a special treat, a drawing will be held at 9:30 p.m. to pick the winners of this year's Winter Carnival prizes: first prize—a remote-control, twenty-one-inch television set; second prize—a deluxe coffee maker; and third prize—a beautiful quartz wall clock. Additionally, free movie passes will be awarded to twenty-five lucky winners. Just fill out an entry ticket at the door. But remem-

ber: you must be there to enter the drawing and claim
your prize!

So that we can make appropriate arrangements
for the smorgasbord and other refreshments, please let
Jim Dixon in the Personnel Office know whether you plan
to attend and whether you will bring a guest.

Do come and enjoy a fun-filled night on December 9. We'll see you then!

Appointment

Subject: Appointment re Baxter Account

Phil, could you meet me in my office at 2 p.m.
on Wednesday, March 17, to discuss the Baxter Account?
I have information concerning their new campaign that
will interest you.

Please let me know by March 14 whether this
time is convenient. Thanks very much.

Credit Information

Subject: A-1 Photographers

A-1 Photographers has an excellent credit
standing with our firm. It has maintained an account with
us for nearly twenty years, with monthly purchases av-
eraging $250. Based on our experience, I would not hesi-
tate to recommend it as a credit customer.

If I can offer any additional information, do let
me know.

Evaluation

Subject: Arnold Frost

Enclosed are the employee-performance-rating scorecards for Arnold Frost: (1) education, (2) skills, and (3) personal attributes.

EDUCATION: Frost is a graduate of Commercial City Business College and has completed several writing correspondence courses and one photography correspondence course.

SKILLS: He has excellent bookkeeping and word-processing skills, with two years of computer training. His editorial skills are moderately well developed, and his knowledge of photography is extensive.

PERSONAL ATTRIBUTES: He is a pleasant, courteous, and well-groomed employee who makes a good impression on others. He is hardworking, attentive to details, and receptive to challenging situations.

SUMMARY: Davis's scores are above average in most categories in which his performance was rated. His high ratings qualify him for further advancement in his department.

Let me know, Ellen, if you need further information.

Instructions

Subject: Class-Registration Procedures

Effective August 1, we will follow a new procedure in registering employees in our training seminars. Previously, we collected updated educational-background and job-experience information on the first day of class. Hereafter, this will be the procedure:

1. Post a notice on the bulletin board that enrollees must fill out a data sheet on or before the day of registration and submit it to the training office.

2. Place a supply of data sheets in each department and in obvious common areas such as the entrance to the cafeteria.

3. As data sheets are collected, attach them to the employee's registration form.

We hope this procedure—giving prospective enrollees an opportunity to fill out their data sheets in advance—will (1) facilitate the enrollment process on registration day and (2) give instructors a chance to learn more about their students' needs before classes begin.

If you have any questions, please let me know. Thanks very much for your help.

Order

Subject: Reprint Order for Stationery

Please reprint the following items for Beehive Accessories, Inc. Negatives and plates are on file in your establishment.

(1) 1,000, 8½ × 11, 20# Beehive letterhead, 25% cotton, pearl white Century stock

(2) 1,000, #10 matching-stock letterhead envelopes

(3) 2,500, 5½ × 8½, standard carbonless, 3-part, 3-color Beehive invoice forms

(4) 2,500, #5⅝ matching-stock invoice window envelopes

Sample copies of each item are attached. We will need this order by Friday, April 29, 1986. Please phone me immediately at 761-8029 if any delay is anticipated.

Thank you.

Reminder

Subject: Sales Meeting Moved to January 11

This is a reminder that our sales-meeting date has been changed from Monday, January 7, to Friday, January 11, 1986. The time and place are the same: 10 a.m. in the company presentation room.

See you on January 11.

Report

Subject: Conference Proceedings

This is the status of the papers for our twenty-third proceedings:

1. Four of the nineteen papers are late.

2. The fifteen papers that have been received are copyedited and typemarked and are being reviewed by the chairman one last time before submitting them to the typesetter on Monday, May 1.

3. Members of the proceedings committee are contacting speakers to determine the status of the four missing papers.

4. The late speakers will be given a firm deadline for submission: May 10. Any papers not in by then will not be part of the bound proceedings (although they may be printed separately as handouts in the speakers' sessions).

5. Other work on the proceedings—cover design, proofreading, and so on—is tightly scheduled and will be monitored closely until completion.

Let me know, Dave, if you need any further information. Next report: April 15.

Request

Subject: Permission to Quote from <u>Writer's Aid</u>

      I am preparing a textbook about nonfiction writing scheduled for publication by ABC Publishers in 1987 and would like to include the last paragraph on page 320 of <u>Writer's Aid</u> by Janet Seely.

      May I have your permission to use this material in my forthcoming book and in future revisions and editions thereof, including nonexclusive world rights in all languages? These rights will in no way restrict republication of your material in any other form by you or others authorized by you. If you do not control these rights in their entirety, I would appreciate it if you would let me know to whom else I should write.

      For your convenience, the following form may be used to grant your permission and indicate your preferred credit line. A copy of this letter is enclosed for your files.

      I will greatly appreciate your consent. Thank you very much.

CREDIT LINE:_____

_____

_____

I (we) grant permission for the use requested above.

_____   _____

Signature   Date

_____   _____

Name   Address

_____

Transmittal

Subject: February Production Data

Here are the statistics you requested, Fred. The enclosed graphs show not only the February data but data for the past four months and for each February during the past three years.

Hope this will help you. Let me know if you need more information.

FORM-LETTER
EFFECTIVENESS CHECKLIST

	Yes	*No*
Is the form letter designed so that a typist can make typed fill-ins easily?	( )	( )
Has a test been made to see whether a file copy of the letter is actually needed or whether the prescribed number of copies can be reduced?	( )	( )
Is the letter easily understood on the first reading?	( )	( )
Is it free of old-fashioned letter language, such as "reference is made to," "you are advised that," and "examination of our records discloses"?	( )	( )
Has a "usage" test been made to see whether it is practical to carry a printed stock?	( )	( )
Does the letter concern a routine business or informational matter?	( )	( )
Is there a mark to show the typist where to begin the address so that it will show in the window of an envelope?	( )	( )

	Yes	No
Will the supply on hand be used up in a few months' time?	( )	( )
Is the letter identified in any way, for example, by a number printed in one of the corners?	( )	( )
If you were the person receiving the form letter, would you consider it effective and attractive?	( )	( )
Has a test been made of typed letters to see whether it is practical to replace any of them with form letters?	( )	( )
Has provision been made for reviewing all requests for form letters to make sure that unnecessary, poorly written, and poorly designed letters do not slip into print?	( )	( )
Do you have standards that you expect all form letters to meet?	( )	( )
Are form letters put into use by written instructions explaining when they are to be used, enclosures (if any) that should be made, and carbon-copy requirements?	( )	( )
Do you have a systematic way of numbering form letters?	( )	( )
When form letters become obsolete, are immediate instructions issued to discontinue their use and to remove old stock from supply cabinets and desk?	( )	( )

Source: National Archives and Records Service, Records Management Division, General Services Administration, Washington, D.C.

NOTE: A checkmark in the "No" column indicates the need for corrective action.

CHECKLIST FOR EDITING CORRESPONDENCE

	Yes	No
Letter describes reason for writing	( )	( )
States what information is needed	( )	( )
Gives information that reader requested	( )	( )
Gives full details reader needs	( )	( )
Has verified facts and figures	( )	( )
Indicates what action reader should take	( )	( )
Thanks reader for interest	( )	( )
Expresses appreciation for something received	( )	( )
Expresses apology for problem or error	( )	( )
Presents case honestly and objectively	( )	( )
Repeats facts in confirming something	( )	( )
Asks for prompt reply	( )	( )
Does not mix business with condolences, congratulations, and so on	( )	( )
Is tactful and considerate of reader's feelings	( )	( )
Does not talk down to reader	( )	( )
Offers encouragement, suggestions, or solution	( )	( )
Offers incentive and is persuasive	( )	( )
Leaves door open for further contact	( )	( )
Has sincere and natural tone	( )	( )
Uses friendly, conversational language	( )	( )

	Yes	No
Uses active voice	( )	( )
Is specific and straightforward	( )	( )
Has correct and effective word choice	( )	( )
Has correct and consistent spelling	( )	( )
Has correct and consistent punctuation	( )	( )
Has correct and consistent capitalization	( )	( )
Uses correct grammar and parts of speech	( )	( )
Avoids cliches, irrelevancies, pretentious language, vogue words, jargon, gobbledygook, euphemisms, trite expressions, and discriminatory expressions	( )	( )
Does not abbreviate unnecessarily or improperly	( )	( )
Has a strong, to-the-point opening	( )	( )
Has a strong, effective ending	( )	( )
Has smooth transitions between sentences and paragraphs	( )	( )
Uses correct form of address, salutation, complimentary close, and signature line	( )	( )
Is prepared in proper letter (or memo) format	( )	( )

NOTE: To use this general checklist, first put an asterisk by each item that would apply to the type of letter you are writing. For example, "Thanks reader for interest" would apply to a letter of reply to an inquiry but not to a letter of condolence. Then review your draft and mark each asterisked item yes or no. Be brutally honest. If your letter sounds stiff and cold, for instance, mark both "Has sincere and natural tone" and "Uses friendly, conversational language" no. Unless you have some reason for being stern (such as a final, legal collection letter), rewrite your draft to soften and relax its tone.

4. MANUSCRIPT PREPARATION AND PRODUCTION

The road from concept to printed product can be long and difficult. In between you may face many perplexing tasks such as selecting the right format for your work, securing permission to quote others, editing and proofreading what you have written, and arranging for copyright protection; you may have to set up supporting material such as tables and footnotes and prepare an index. The most impressive writing style and superb example of grammatical accuracy will be lost if your message is not formatted and typed or typeset properly. Because writing and production are so closely related, manuscript preparation and production should rate high among a careful writer's concerns.

MANUSCRIPT-PREPARATION GUIDELINES

ORGANIZATION

You will save time if you plan ahead and have all written materials and typing or word-processing tools available before you begin preparing the final draft of your manuscript. Determine the format you want to use; be certain that you have enough paper, typewriter or printer ribbons, diskettes, and other typing and correction supplies on hand. Double-check your rough draft for completeness and sequence of material. Ask your publisher or employer about the desired format, number of copies needed, and other requirements. Check your schedule for final tasks, including mailing time, to insure that you meet your deadline. Review the material in this chapter as a final reminder of things to do.

FORMAT

Unless you are given style and format instructions and special paper to use, prepare your manuscript on one side of white bond paper, 8½ by 11 inches, 20-pound substance. Do *not* use erasable paper, which smudges too easily. Most publishers require an original and one or two copies made on paper similar to that of the original.

Use pica type, which is larger than elite and easier for editors and typesetters to read. Do not use italic, script, or bold (dark, heavy) typefaces. To specify italics, use underlining. See **USE OF ITALICS IN TYPED AND PRINTED MATERIAL** in this chapter. The editor or designer will decide if any material should be in a bold face. Except in the case of table headings or headings that are part of a text paragraph (*run-in heads*), do not underline titles and subheads. Do not type titles and subheads in all capital letters unless it is necessary to distinguish several levels of headings or show that a heading is a separate item from other material.

Double-space everything, including footnotes (you may use additional space around headings and display material).

Use margins of about 1¼ inches on both sides and 1 to 1¼ inches top and bottom. Use 2-inch margins for display material such as mathematical equations. Begin new chapters about 3 inches from the top of the page. Keep lines fairly even, but avoid excessive hyphenation at the end of lines.

Number pages consecutively in the upper right-hand corner. Front matter need not be numbered, except for a preface or foreword, which should be numbered separately from the text. An index also is treated as a separate document in numbering, but a glossary or an appendix is numbered along with the rest of the manuscript. Use numbers and letters for late inserts (for example, page 91, 91a, 91b, 91c).

For examples of specific formats, see **BASIC LETTER FORMATS** and **BASIC MEMO FORMATS** in Chapter 3 and **MODEL FOOTNOTES, BIBLIOGRAPHIES, AND CREDIT LINES; GUIDELINES FOR PREPARING TABLES; PRINCIPAL PARTS OF A BOOK; PRINCIPAL PARTS OF FORMAL AND INFORMAL REPORTS; PRESS RELEASE CHARACTERISTICS;** and **RESUME FORMATS** in this chapter.

WRITING AND EDITING

Follow the recommendations in **BASIC STEPS IN THE WRITING PROCESS** in Chapter 1. For guidance in specific areas such as writing techniques and grammar, review all of chapters 1 and 2. Also check the various tables in this chapter, such as **USE OF ITALICS IN TYPED AND PRINTED MATERIAL, USE OF QUOTED MATERIAL, CHART OF PROOFREADER MARKS, SAMPLE PAGE OF EDITED AND TYPEMARKED MANUSCRIPT, EDITING CHECKLIST,** and **INDEX-PREPARATION PROCE-**

DURES. Make as many changes and corrections as possible in the manuscript-typing stage. Once your copy is typeset, changes become costly. After all editing is finished and the sequence of your material is established, verify cross-references (wording of the title or subhead, chapter number, and so on) and compare footnote numbering in the text with that in the notes section. Avoid frequent references to specific pages, but if necessary, type "see page 000" and fill in the correct number later when page proofs are available.

LIBEL

Libel is a false or malicious statement in writing that injures a person's reputation; for example, reflections on a person's competence or honesty may be libelous. Consider the danger of libelous statements *before* you complete and submit your manuscript. Discuss the matter with your editor if there is a potential problem. If you have any doubts, check with an attorney. Also, examine your work for unintentional slurs against race or religion and attacks on professional groups or businesses. Some writing, although not legally threatening, may nevertheless offend individuals or groups. Review the suggestions for avoiding biased remarks in **NONDISCRIMI-NATORY-WRITING GUIDELINES** in Chapter 1.

INVASION OF PRIVACY

Several right-to-privacy statutes have been passed since the subject first received attention in 1890. Most states have at least one statute, although the various statutes are not uniform from state to state. Examples of acts that invade privacy are casting a person in a false light, or putting something accurate in an inaccurate context; revealing truthful but embarrassing private information about someone; and creating fictional dialogue for someone without basis. Because of the potential problems in this area, writers should proceed with caution in matters involving private parties who are described, photographed, quoted, or otherwise portrayed in printed material. It is not only prudent but often essential to obtain releases for use of photographs and other material; see **RELEASE FORMS** in Chapter 5. To avoid difficulties, including possible lawsuits, read the applicable statutes before your work is published. Discuss any doubtful situations with the publisher or your employer, and seek the advice of an attorney if you have not yet resolved all questionable matters.

ILLUSTRATIONS

Artwork and photographs: Each piece should be prepared on a separate sheet and marked with the text page number where the figure is first mentioned. If there are numerous illustrations, submit a separately numbered illustration manuscript. If you have only a few pages, insert copies of the illustration sheets at the end of the appropriate chapter(s) and number the pages as part of the text manuscript. Keep the original drawings and photographs apart from the rest of the manuscript.

Photographs, commonly referred to as halftones (see Glossary), are best submitted to a printer as black-and-white glossy prints, 8 by 10 inches. Submit color prints only if the printed material, such as an annual report, requires full color. If you want only a portion of the photograph to appear in the printed document, put crop marks (see Glossary) in the white outer border with a grease pencil to show the area you want to use.

Line drawings (see Glossary) such as charts, graphs, diagrams, and other line artwork do not have tonal values like a photograph. They may consist of pen-and-ink hand drawings or computer-rendered drawings. Commercial artwork, often prepared by an artist, must consist of sharp, black lines on a clean, white background. Complex line drawings may contain

Benday (see Glossary) shaded patterns and other techniques to add variety. These variations are useful in graphic presentations such as pie charts, bar charts, column charts, and other pictorial line illustrations.

In the case of both halftones and line drawings, mark instructions for the printer on tissue or acetate overlays (see Glossary). But do *not* write on the surface of the photograph or drawing. Instructions may include the size to which the item must be reduced (for example, from 8 by 10 inches to 2 by 2½ inches—a reduction of 75 percent); whether the item is to bleed (be printed off the edge of the paper without a margin); the position, or page, in the manuscript where the item is to appear; and so on. The more information you give the printer, the greater the likelihood that the finished product will meet your expectations.

Tables: Type small, unnumbered tables where they belong in the text discussion. Type large tables on separate sheets and insert them at the end of the appropriate chapter(s) or prepare a separate table manuscript if you have a large number of tables. For details about typing tables, see **GUIDELINES FOR PREPARING TABLES** in this chapter.

Specifically mention each piece in the text discussion, for example, "See Figure 3" or "See Table 10." Number the tables and figures consecutively throughout the manuscript (Table 1, Table 2 . . . Table 25) or by chapter (Figure 1-1, Figure 1-2 . . . Figure 1-6; Figure 2-1, Figure 2-2 . . . Figure 2-17).

Type all figure legends, source notes, and other material to be typeset on a separate sheet, whether you or an outside artist or the publisher is preparing the artwork. Double-check facts and statistics for accuracy and eliminate "cosmetic" material—illustrations that are not necessary and do not significantly supplement and support the text discussion. Although color is essential in some material, such as an annual report, do not submit color artwork and photographs for a black-and-white publication.

When you want to reprint previously published material, ask the copyright owner or original source of the material for a clear, sharp, reproducible copy of the table or figure you want to use. (Ask your employer or publisher about preparation requirements for all drawings and photographs.) Tables and figures that use material from another source should have a source note positioned immediately following the last line of the illustration, before any table or figure footnotes. Often copyright owners supply the credit lines they want you to use. For more information about the use of previously printed material, see PERMISSIONS on page 141.

NOTES AND BIBLIOGRAPHIES

Type notes double-spaced on a separate page at the end of each chapter and number them consecutively within the chapter. For style suggestions, see **KINDS OF NOTES AND REFERENCE CITATIONS** and **MODEL FOOTNOTES, BIBLIOGRAPHIES, AND CREDIT LINES** in this chapter. Type the bibliography double-spaced in a separate section at the end of the manuscript. Compare each footnote to the corresponding entry in the bibliography. Although the style of each differs, the facts in a note should be identical to the information in a bibliography entry.

Check the consistency of note numbering in the text discussion with the number sequence in the notes section. You may separate straight references from expository notes, using arabic numbers for the reference notes and small alphabet letters or asterisks for the expository notes. The name-date style (for example, Edwards 1980), often used in the social and natural sciences, does not use numbers or letters; in-text citations refer instead to the author's last name and the year of publication.

PERMISSIONS

Write to the copyright owner when you want to quote or reprint text, tables, figures, or other material from another source. A sample permissions request is shown in **MODEL MEMOS, Request,** in Chapter 3. To avoid last-minute delays, write for permissions as soon as you know what outside material you want to use. Titles and ideas are not copyrightable, but an author's words and the development and treatment of an idea are copyrightable.

Ask your employer or publisher for house specifications concerning the number of words, scattered throughout your manuscript, that you may quote from any source without requesting permission to use the material (under one hundred words for an article and under three hundred words for a book are the guidelines used by some organizations). Whether or not permission is required, you must include a text footnote or a table or figure source note giving credit to the original author and copyright owner. See **USE OF QUOTED MATERIAL; KINDS OF NOTES AND REFERENCE CITATIONS; MODEL FOOTNOTES, BIBLIOGRAPHIES, AND CREDIT LINES;** and **COPYRIGHTING** in this chapter.

TYPEWRITER PREPARATION

Follow the guidelines concerning margins, type size, and other specifications discussed in FORMAT (page 135). Use clean type bars; fresh, dark ribbons; and erasing materials that avoid or minimize distortions of the typing. Make duplicate copies by a clear photographic means (for example, bond copier), not by the use of carbon paper. Type the manuscript in a neat, clear, legible manner, with typed rather than hand-written inserts and corrections if possible. When you must insert material such as mathematical symbols by hand, use pen and ink; clearly *print* any words or sentences you insert by hand.

Although editing should be done before you type your final manuscript copy, when you must make a correction, use the symbols for corrections and insertions shown in **CHART OF PROOFREADER MARKS** in this chapter. Never type an insertion sideways on the page. Type it so that the lines of type inserted run horizontally the same as the other typed lines. Retype a page if it is noticeably marred by corrections and has numerous insertions. When necessary, you may insert a large block of new material by typing it on a separate sheet placed immediately after the page on which you want it to appear. If the insert goes on page 11, number the new sheet 11a and type at the top "Insert on page 11." At the appropriate place on page 11, make a note in the margin to "Insert page 11a here."

Some typewriters have lift-off correction tapes; separate correction tape, fluids, and erasers are also available in office-supply stores. Other typewriters, such as the advanced electronic models, have memories and certain capabilities (for example, automatic centering) similar to those of a computer.

Prepare front matter and end matter in the order described in **PRINCIPAL PARTS OF A BOOK** and **PRINCIPAL PARTS OF FORMAL AND INFORMAL REPORTS** in this chapter. In all matters of style, format, and sequence of material, follow the requirements of your employer or publisher if known; refer to the guidelines in this chapter when no house requirements are available.

COMPUTER OR WORD PROCESSOR PREPARATION

Many of the guidelines mentioned in TYPEWRITER PREPA-RATION (pp. 141–42) apply to manuscript preparation by a computer or word processor (a dedicated computer). Specific procedures vary depending on the type of hardware (the particular computer or word processor) and software (the particular word-processing program that enables you to enter, edit, and print out copy). In all cases, though, you must make decisions concerning format, sequence of material, and other specifications described here. Your employer or publisher may ask you to submit diskettes in addition to two or three paper copies of the manuscript.

Instead of using correction materials and retyping pages each time you make a change or correction, you will do your editing by typing corrections on a typewriterlike keyboard, with the images appearing on a televisionlike screen. By pushing special keys you can delete, insert, and move words, blocks of copy, and even complete chapters. Depending on the equipment you have, the information you type will probably be stored on a small, flat diskette, a permanent hard disk, or a cassette tape.

Manuscript preparation is usually simplified with a computer, since manual typewriter tasks such as carriage return at the end of each line of type are handled automatically by the computer. Indentations, spacing, and other format details are efficiently handled by entering (typing) the specifications you want and then pushing certain designated keys. The computer will indent all paragraphs at once, insert a line space between all paragraphs at once, and instantly do various other tasks for you.

To make changes in your manuscript later (to edit), you simply insert the appropriate diskette (if that is what your equipment uses), type the name of the file you want to locate (the name you gave to a particular chapter or section in a particular manuscript), and push the designated keys, and the material you want to work on will appear on the monitor (the televisionlike screen). Backup (duplicate) copies of disk files are recommended.

After all final changes and corrections are made and you have entered the proper format specifications (margins, position of page numbers, and so on) into the computer memory, the printer will type one or more copies of each page automatically—what you prepared by keyboard and saw on the monitor will be transferred to paper.

MAILING

Some writers mail their original and duplicate manuscripts in separate packages to avoid the possible loss of everything in one occurrence. Mail small pieces such as an article in an envelope by first-class mail. Depending on the deadline, you may send a large manuscript in a box at the lower special-fourth-class-manuscript rate or the faster but more expensive priority-mail rate. For added protection you may send it by insured or registered priority mail. Ask at your local post office about rates, packaging requirements for each class, and delivery time. Also review **POSTAL REGULATIONS** in Chapter 5. When time is especially short, use the Postal Service's Express Mail class or one of the overnight courier services.

All manuscripts, except one of two or three pages, should be mailed flat, with cardboard backing to protect them. Unless you are sending a manuscript out on speculation, enclose all pertinent material such as copies of your permissions letters and the replies to them. Use sturdy backing for artwork and photographs. Manuscripts must also be unbound, although you should place rubber bands around the loose pages of a large work or use paper clips to secure the pages of a short piece (do not staple small works).

Enclose a brief transmittal letter stating what is being sent, for which publication it is intended, and that a stamped, self-addressed envelope is enclosed for its return (or that postage stamps and a mailing-address label are enclosed in the case of a large work). End the letter with a brief "thank you." When the manuscript is sent at the lower fourth-class rate, add first-class postage for the letter and write "Letter Enclosed" on the package. For manuscripts sent out of country, enclose International Reply Coupons (purchased at the post office) instead of postage.

Follow the same procedure when mailing to a literary agent, but remember that some publishers and agents will not read unsolicited manuscripts. Addresses of publishers and agents are available in directories such as *Literary Market Place* (R. R. Bowker) and *Writer's Market* (Writer's Digest).

USE OF ITALICS IN TYPED AND PRINTED MATERIAL

EMPHASIS

Use italics sparingly for emphasis. Do not italicize entire sentences or passages, except when you are copying the italics in quoted material.

Example: The situation is not only undesirable; it is *dangerous*.

WORDS USED AS WORDS

Use italics for words referred to as words and for certain letters used as words or letters.

Example: the word *government;* the letters *r* and *t;* C major; Mr. T; S-shape; *hackneyed,* meaning "trite"

FOREIGN TERMS

Use italics only for *unfamiliar* foreign words. But do not use italics for proper names. See **FAMILIAR FOREIGN WORDS** in Chapter 5.
Example: de escribir; mea culpa; Chofu (Japanese city)

LEGAL CASES

Use italics for legal cases. The *v.* or *vs.* (versus) may be roman or italic.
Example: Finley v. *Stone;* the *Finley* case

CRAFT AND VESSELS

Use italics for names of ships and other craft. Do not use italics for preceding abbreviations or for types of craft or vessels.
Example: USS *Nautilus;* HMS *Dominion; Voyager 2;* Boeing 727

SCIENTIFIC NAMES

Use italics for genera, subgenera, species, and subspecies. Do not use italics for larger divisions such as phyla, classes, orders, families, and tribes.
Example: the species *Spizella pusilla;* the family Fringillidae

PUBLICATIONS, ARTWORK, AND MUSICAL COMPOSITIONS

Use italics for titles of publications such as newspapers, periodicals, and books; titles of collections of poetry and long poems; and titles of plays and motion pictures; for titles of paintings, drawings, statues, and other works of art; and for titles of operas, oratorios, motets, tone poems, and other long musical compositions as well as descriptive titles of long musical works. Do not italicize traditional or descriptive titles (such as Mona Lisa) or musical works identified by a key or number (such as Piano Concerto no. 5).

Example: *Newsweek* magazine; Dante's poem *The Divine Comedy;* the Broadway play *Cats;* the film *Star Wars;* Rodin's sculpture *The Thinker;* Beethoven's *Emperor* Concerto; Handel's oratorio *Messiah*

NOTE: In typed material, underscore words that should be italicized. See also **USE OF QUOTED MATERIAL, ITALICS**, in this chapter.

USE OF QUOTED MATERIAL

QUOTATION MARKS

Use double quotation marks ('') at the beginning and end of quoted words and at the beginning of each new quoted paragraph, unless a quoted passage is set as an indented block of copy. See **EXTRACTS**.

Example: ''Place commas and a final period *inside* quotation marks. Place other punctuation such as a semicolon inside quotation marks only when it is a part of the matter quoted''; otherwise, as shown here, place it *outside*.

Use single quotation marks (') to enclose quotations within quotations.

Example: "Insert the phrase 'I will appreciate your help.' "

ITALICS

Underscore words that are italicized in the material you are quoting. When you want to emphasize something in the quoted material, you may underscore it also if you include the words "emphasis mine," "emphasis added," "italics mine," or "italics added" in brackets after the passage or in parentheses at the end of the quotation.

Example: "Use italics *sparingly* [emphasis mine] in your work." "Use italics *sparingly* in your work" (emphasis mine).

ERRORS

Copy errors in quoted material exactly as they appear. To indicate that the errors were in the original material, type *sic* in brackets after the incorrect word(s).

Example: "We were lately [*sic*] in arriving."

OMISSION

Use points of ellipsis, or dots (. . .), to show omitted words or paragraphs. Put a space between the last word and the first dot unless the first dot represents a period, and put a space between each dot and the next. Use three dots for words omitted in the middle of a sentence or at the beginning of a sentence or to show that the end of a sentence is grammatically incomplete. You may also use a separate line of several dots or asterisks about five spaces apart to show omission of several paragraphs. See EXTRACTS for an example of omission at the beginning of the first and succeeding paragraphs.

Example: "Use points of ellipsis . . . to show omitted words. . . . Use three dots for words omitted in the middle or at the beginning of a sentence and four dots for words, sentences, or paragraphs omitted at the end of a grammatically complete sentence. . . . and use four dots to show the omission of words both at the end of one sentence and the beginning of the next sentence."

EXTRACTS

Type quoted material of eight or more lines in a separate, indented block of copy. You may indent both the left and right margins of the extract (at least five spaces) or the left margin only. In manuscript copy, double-space the extract the same as the other text material, with an additional line space between paragraphs and above and below the extract. Do *not* use beginning and ending quotation marks with an extract (typing it as an indented block shows that it is a quote). If there are single quotation marks in the passage being quoted, change them to double marks in the extract.

Example: Writers should heed the following advice in using quotation marks:

> Use quotation marks to enclose . . . quotations of writ-ten or spoken material, but do not enclose *yes* or *no* except in direct discourse. . . . In typeset material, underscored words are set in italics. . . .
>
> . . . and do not enclose slang in quotation marks. . . . do not enclose words following the expression *so-called* in quotation marks [unless such marks appear in the passage you are quoting].

In this example, the entire left margin is indented, but the right margin is the same as the rest of the text. The words in brackets are comments that did *not* appear in the original passage but were added later by the person who was quoting the material.

Notice that the first sentence is not indented because it falls in the middle of the first paragraph quoted. Since it is typed flush left, it is not necessary to precede that sentence with three dots to show omission of the beginning of the paragraph. The second paragraph is indented and opens with three dots to show that words are omitted at the beginning of a sentence that does *not* open that paragraph.

The four dots at the end of the first paragraph indicate the omission of words, sentences, or paragraphs between it and the second paragraph.

NOTE: See also **RULES OF PUNCTUATION**, QUOTA-TION MARKS, in Chapter 1.

KINDS OF NOTES AND REFERENCE CITATIONS

FOOTNOTES

Footnotes placed at the bottoms of pages where they are cited in the text must be numbered consecutively throughout an article, a report, or a chapter in a longer document. The numbers preceding the footnote copy may be set as superscript (raised) numbers, but in contemporary writing they are more often set on line (aligned with the note text). Corresponding note numbers in the main text material, however, should be set as superscripts and placed *outside* end-of-sentence punctuation, for example: "Information in the article was misleading in the opinion of the council."[1] Avoid middle-of-sentence numbering in the text, and do not place note numbers at the ends of chapter titles, subheads, or other display heads.

Some writers separate expository (discussion) footnotes from reference (source) footnotes. Expository notes are then lettered (a, b, c) or given a sequence of symbols (*, **, ***) and are placed at the foot of appropriate text pages; the reference notes are numbered and collected in a notes section at the end of each chapter or at the end of a book or an article (see ENDNOTES).

Always renumber notes and corresponding text numbers when you add or delete footnotes. Number table and figure footnotes apart from text notes. See **GUIDELINES FOR PREPARING TABLES** in this chapter.

To avoid long lists of repetitive notes consisting only of different page numbers or ibid., give a numbered note with full reference data the first time cited, but add a statement to that note such as "Page numbers for further references to this work will be cited in the text." If the text has alternate page citations to more than one work, include a short title or the last name of the author with page numbers. For example: "White then amended his decision (*Court Decisions*, 61)"; "Black concurred (*Cases*, 112)."

ENDNOTES

When footnotes are collected at the end of an article, a report, or a chapter in a larger document, they are called endnotes, although the list may be titled simply Notes. These note sections may consist of reference notes only, with expository notes placed at the foot of the appropriate text pages, or they may be combination notes, including both discussion and source within each note. The style is the same for both bottom-of-page footnotes and endnotes.

Very long notes are best set as combination endnotes rather than as footnotes at the bottom of text pages. However, since some readers fail to check endnotes regularly for supporting text comments, be certain that material essential for clarity is stated in the text. Whether you use combination endnotes or separate endnotes and expository notes, follow the guidelines for numbering and citing page numbers in the text given in FOOTNOTES.

UNNUMBERED NOTES

Some notes do not relate to items in the text discussion but are general notes acknowledging someone's contribution or referring to the source of the entire article, chapter, or other division. A source note extending credit should be set as an unnumbered footnote at the bottom of the first page or preceding a list of numbered endnotes. If a copyright notice is included, the note is best positioned at the bottom of the opening page. Copyrighted material must include proper copyright notice and permission to use the material in question. See **COPYRIGHTING** and **MANUSCRIPT-PREPARATION GUIDELINES**, PERMISSIONS, in this chapter.

REFERENCE LISTS

Instead of using numbered notes, you may use an author-date system of citation. This system requires an alphabetical list of sources, with references to the sources given in parentheses in the text, for example: "Editing is therefore simplified" (Smith 1980, 3:51). The notation 3:51 refers to volume 3, page 51. If author Smith has two or three 1980 works on the reference list, specify one as 1980a, another as 1980b, and so on. Position the works alphabetically on the reference list before you add the letters to the years. If two or more Smiths are on the reference list, you will have to give each

Smith's first name in the author-date citation, for example: (J. B. Smith 1980a, 142).

Since the alphabetical reference list consists only of sources, expository notes must be placed at the bottom of the appropriate text pages or in a separate notes section preceding the reference list. The reference list may be titled Bibliography, References, Works Cited, or any other appropriate title. A list titled Select (or Selected) Bibliography would not be appropriate, since it implies that not all works cited in the text are included in the list. You may also have one list titled References or Works Cited and a separate list titled Bibliography (or Select Bibliography).

The author-date citation style is most popular in the natural and social sciences, but it is an easy-to-use, an easy-to-type (or typeset), and a practical system that can—and should—be used in other fields.

NOTE: See **MODEL FOOTNOTES, BIBLIOGRAPHIES, AND CREDIT LINES** for examples of the notes described here.

MODEL FOOTNOTES, BIBLIOGRAPHIES, AND CREDIT LINES

Footnotes

1. Eric Meade and Marshall Randolph, *Printing and Mailing: Pitfalls and Pratfalls*, 2 vols. (New York: Addison Hill & Co., 1981), 1:413.

2. Ibid., 131.

3. Jennifer Platt, "Editing," *Booklover's Digest* 4, no. 23 (April 1985): 13–14; idem, "Writing," *Journalism Today*, 6 September 1973, 11–15.

4. Meade and Randolph, *Printing and Mailing*, 2:305.

5. Platt, "Writing," 13.

6. John Burnett, "Editing," in *Editor's Handbook*, ed. Wilma Alden (Chicago: Editorial Publishers, 1979), 44.

7. David Eaton, comp., *Publishing*, Printers' Society Bulletin no. 91 (Washington, D.C., 1975).

8. Oscar Finley, *Short Stories*, vol. 2 of *Complete Works* (London, 1889).

9. Dennis McKay, *Art and Writing* (1920; reprint, Los Angeles: Art Books, 1973), 207.

10. Jeanne Tremaine, "Proofreading," *Production Journal*, 2d ser., 8 (November 1950): 16–17.

11. Samuel Hartstein, "A Study of Writers: 1820–1920" (Ph.D. diss., Benton University, 1980), 100–101.

12. Miriam Elso, review of *Advertising*, by Henry Sun, *Modern Reviews* 82 (June 1985): 41.

13. William McConnell to Helena Frost, 16 December 1917, William McConnell Manuscripts, File X042-17, Box 91, Public Library, Los Angeles (hereafter cited as McConnell MSS).

14. Editorial, *New York Times*, 8 August 1982.

15. McConnell MSS.

Standard Bibliography

Benjamin, Walter; J. F. Devane; and Lois Porter. *La auteur*.
    1930. Reprint. Concord, N.H.: Northern Printers, 1976.

————. *Modern Writing*. Vol. 3. Portland, Oreg.: Western Printing Co., 1962. Microfiche.

Brett, Lydia. "Writing Tools." *Author's Journal* 3 (1985): 4–5.

Editorial Society. *Survey*. 3 vols. Phoenix, 1974.

Greenley, Paul S. Review of *Handwriting Analysis*, by M. T. Ott. *Penmanship Quarterly*, 14 March 1981, 32.

Hallett, Diana, ed. *Writers' Anthology*. 2d ed. New York: History Publications, 1979.

Ortega, Rita. *Western Authors*. California Monographs, vol. 11, nos. 2–3. San Francisco: Oceanside Press, 1985.

————. *Western Artists*. Newark, N.J.: Global Press, forthcoming.

Reference List

Jones, Julia. 1980a. "Literature." In *New Works*, edited by Mary Miida, 211–12. New Orleans: Library Press.

————. 1980b. *Photojournalism*. 16 mm, 30 min. Distributed by Photo Films Co., Little Rock.

Shakespeare, William. 1902. *Plays*. Neusome Classical Library.

Sharpe, Cecila. 1983. "Editorial Tools." Department of Literature, Central University, Des Moines. Photocopy.

Tonnato, Escela. 1979. "Law in Writing." Paper presented at the annual meeting of the International Writers' Group, Denver, February.

U.S. Congress, Senate. Committee on Energy. 1976. *Hearings on the Energy Program*. 94th Cong., 2d sess. Committee Print 13.

Worster, Drew. 1980. "A History of Printing." Ph.D. dissertation, Eastern College.

Credit Lines

This study was supported by Grant OV-71-UT639, Regional Science Institute, Cincinnati, Ohio.

I gratefully acknowledge the assistance of Lynda Norton and Jane Costello in the preparation of this chapter.

Reprinted with permission of ABC Publishers from *Writing Today,* by Robert Salt. Copyright 1985 by Robert Salt.

Adapted from *Editor's Workbook,* ed. Louis Jeffries (New York: New Printing Company, 1979), 209–10, by permission of the author and publisher. Copyright 1979 by Louis Jeffries.

Portions of this chapter were first published in "Art Notes," *Art Digest* 6, no. 24 (1961): 11. Reprinted with permission.

NOTE: The reference list, with dates immediately after the authors' names, is used with an author-date citation system. Credit lines are usually set at the bottom of opening pages as unnumbered source notes and acknowledgments. See also **GUIDELINES FOR PREPARING TABLES** in this chapter for examples of table footnote style. For descriptions of the various citation styles, see **KINDS OF NOTES AND REFERENCE CITATIONS** in this chapter.

GUIDELINES FOR PREPARING TABLES

Principal Parts of Tables

NUMBER

Usually, when you have more than one table in a manuscript, it is necessary to number each one. Some tables, however, are so brief and simple (perhaps only a couple of lines) that a table title and number are unwarranted. Also, books consisting solely of tables such as an almanac are commonly prepared without a numbering system. But when you use table numbers, type the number flush left, two line spaces above the table title (see **Model Table Format**); when a title is very short, however, you may type the number followed by the title on the same line.

Number the tables, using arabic numerals, consecutively throughout the manuscript (Table 1, Table 2 . . . Table 25), or number them consecutively within each chapter of a large, multiauthor work (Table 1.1, Table 1.2, Table 2.1, Table 2.2); number appendix tables apart from chapter tables (A-1, A-2, B-1, B-2). Use either periods or hyphens in a double enumeration system; the first number or letter is the chapter number or appendix letter, and the second one is the table number.

Always mention *each* table by number (or letter) in the text discussion of your manuscript (for example, "see Table 9.7"); also be certain that tables are arranged in proper order so that they are cited in the proper sequence. (Do not refer to tables 1, 2, and 3 in the text and then skip over to 5 before mentioning number 4.)

Example: Table 2.1

Production of Gold and Silver, 1970—80

Table 2.2. Foreign Currency

TITLE

Type the table title two line spaces beneath the table number (see **Model Table Format**) or following the table number on the same line if the title is very short. Keep titles brief, with explanatory comments confined to footnotes. Select descriptive words that concisely identify (not discuss) the table. Type subheads to a title, such as "In Thousands of Dollars," in parentheses flush left, two line spaces beneath the title Capitalize all important words in the title (for example, Insurance Claims by Sex and Age, 1985). When there are a number of column headings in the table, type a single horizontal rule between the table title and the column headings.

Example: Table A-1

Weights and Measures by Country
(In Metric System Values)

Table A-2. Computer Symbols

HEADINGS

Type a heading above each column in a table, except for the left-hand list (*stub*), which may not need a heading. Make any heading above the stub singular; use singular or plural for the other column headings. Select words that briefly identify the data in the column beneath each heading (for example, Percentage of Claims). Type subheads such as "Millions" and "%" in parentheses at the end of the column heading or on the first line below the main column heading. When more than one level is used (*decked* head), separate the levels with a horizontal rule (see **Model Table Format**). Capitalize all important words in column headings. When there are a number of column headings, type a single horizontal rule beneath the headings to separate them from the table body.

Example: Public   Commercial
             Television   Television
             Viewers   Viewers
             (Millions)   (Millions)

STUB

Type the table stub, the left-hand list of items, flush left (see **Model Table Format**), indenting subheads under a stub item two or three spaces. Indent the word *Total* at the end of the stub two or three spaces more than the word immediately above it. Generally, capitalize only the first word in a stub item.

Example: Republican party
             Democratic party
             Social Democratic party
             Socialist party

BODY

Two or more columns of information next to the stub constitute the body of a table. Double-space all data in the body, whether the data are words or statistics. Generally, center short items in a column; type long items flush left within each column. But align all figures at the decimal point and put commas in numbers of one thousand or more (1,792).

When the figures in a column are of the same type, such as all percentages or all dollars, type the % or $ symbol only after or before the top figure in a column. Use either an extra line space or a ruled line above the final row of figures representing column totals (see **Model Table Format**). When no data are available for a particular item, type a dash (two hyphens) in the appropriate column space. Be certain to explain, in a footnote, any deviations you have made or other discrepancies, for example, when numbers have been rounded off or why the total of percentages in a column does not equal one hundred.

Type a final rule between the body of the table and the footnotes beneath it.

Example: $ 1,942.30
                  16.02
                 191.40
              31,000.00
                   0.17
                   --
                 234.88

SOURCE NOTE

Type a table source note flush left, double-spaced, beneath the body of the table when you want to identify and properly credit the source of the information you are using (see **Model Table Format**). If permission is required to use the table data, write to the copyright owner. When a copyright owner specifies the wording you must use in the source note, type it exactly as it is given to you. See **MODEL FOOTNOTES, BIBLIOGRAPHIES, AND CREDIT LINES** in this chapter for sample notes.

FOOTNOTES

Type general table notes and other footnotes flush left, double-spaced, immediately beneath the table source note. A broad comment such as a remark about the table in general is usually preceded by the word *Note* rather than by a footnote number or letter. Always use a general note, not a numbered or lettered footnote, with remarks pertaining to the table title.

Use numbers, letters, or symbols (1, 2, 3; a, b, c; *, **, ***) with footnotes referring to specific items in the table body. Table footnotes preceded by numbers, letters, or symbols are typed beneath the source note or beneath the general note, if there is one (see **Model Table Format**). Type the number, letter, or symbol preceding the footnote information on line (not raised), followed by a period. But type the corresponding number, letter, or symbol in the table body as a raised element (*superscript*). See **MODEL FOOTNOTES, BIBLIOGRAPHIES, AND CREDIT LINES** in this chapter for sample notes. Avoid using footnote letters such as *a*, *b*, and *c* in the body of a table already containing other small letters; similarly, avoid using numbers for table footnotes when the table body already has numbers in it.

Model Table Format

Table 1

Participation in Writing Workshops by Type of Writing, 1983–86

| | Percentage of Total Attendance | | | |
	1983	1984	1985	1986
Books				
Fiction[a]	20%	20%	19%	16%
Nonfiction[a]	26	28	29	36
Article	20	21	23	24
Short stories	23	22	19	17
Poetry	11	9	10	7[b]
Totals	100	100	100	100

Source: Sloane Writing Workshops, Sloane Writing Program, Workbook #1 (Prescott, Ariz.: Sloane Educational Programs, Inc., 1982), 17. Reprinted with permission.

Note: The Sloane Writing Workshops is a division of Sloane
Educational Programs, Inc.

a. The decline in fiction-book-writing interest and the increase in nonfiction-book-writing interest in part reflects
additional attention created by Sloane's 1985–86 nonfic-
tion-writing contest.

b. Sloane officials indicated in a personal interview, September 16, 1986, that poetry may be phased out of the program
if participation does not exceed 7 percent in 1987.

PRINCIPAL PARTS
OF FORMAL AND
INFORMAL REPORTS

Principal Report Forms

LETTER OR MEMO

The most informal type of report is a traditional letter or
memo. It may, however, include underscored or capitalized
subheadings as illustrated in **MODEL MEMOS, Evalu-
ation,** in Chapter 3. Although this type of report is written
in a letter or memo format, it should state who authorized
the report (if anyone), the date of authorization, the objective of the report, its scope, and the conclusions or
recommendations. Like any other report, it should introduce
the report topic, logically develop the theme, and provide a
persuasive argument and conclusions. Even if it is merely an
objective, informational report, with no persuasive or sales
effort involved, the data must nevertheless be organized in an
orderly, easy-to-follow sequence.

The discussion should use simple sentences and short paragraphs (as most reports should) and aim for clarity and reader comprehension. See **EDITING CHECKLIST** in this chapter. Whether or not subheads are used in the letter or memo, the principal parts of the discussion should follow the order of topic presentation described in SHORT, INFORMAL REPORT, including an introduction, body, and conclusions and recommendations.

FORM

Some reports are prepared on a printed form, with blanks where you fill in the required data. Examples are expense-report forms and time-study forms. Such forms indicate what information is required and, when necessary, provide instructions for filling in the blanks. Even though a printed form seems less formal than other report styles, you should provide all information that is requested and use correct grammar, with clear, concise statements, the same as you would do for any other type of report.

SHORT, INFORMAL REPORT

The content and style of a short, informal report may resemble a letter or memo report, but it is prepared on plain paper rather than stationery. The transmittal letter or memo that accompanies the report, however, should be prepared on company letterhead. Like any report, the short form must use a businesslike tone and persuasive language (if appropriate); it also should be written with short paragraphs and simple sentences, striving for clarity and readability. Principal parts may include some or all of the following sections, positioned in the order stated:

Preliminary summary: a brief statement (often one or two paragraphs) of the report thesis, the findings, and your conclusions and recommendations.

Introduction: a brief statement (often one to three paragraphs) of the history, objectives, and scope of the report.

Body: the discussion of your topic and a detailed analysis. Following the introduction, you should develop your theme in a logical, step-by-step procedure, presenting the problem, your findings, and your argument and offering whatever documentation (statistics, other reports, and so on) is necessary to support your thesis.

Conclusions and recommendations: a brief statement of the results of your study and suggestions for a plan of action (if appropriate). Keep the conclusion brief and use it to focus effectively on the principal point(s) you want to make to leave the reader with the desired impression. Avoid a summary that merely repeats verbatim the paragraphs in the body of the report.

Appendix: supplementary material such as graphs, tables, charts, and forms. See **MODEL FOOTNOTES, BIBLIOGRAPHIES, AND CREDIT LINES** and **GUIDELINES FOR PREPARING TABLES** in this chapter.

FORMAL REPORT

A formal report has more detail and often more parts than the short, informal report. But the specific parts included may vary from one report to another. Some formal reports, for instance, have no cover; others have no letter of transmittal within the report itself (it is prepared as a separate item in that case). However, long formal reports usually include most of these principal parts in the order shown:

Cover: a special outer wrapper that covers or encloses the pages of the report. It may give the report title, date of the report, name and job title of the preparer, and possibly the company name and location. Some report covers are specially designed and printed and may contain additional information or less information. Others show the information typed in a position similar to that on the title page. See **Model Title Page.**

Flyleaf: a blank page inserted between the cover and the title page.

Title page: the first page of the report. It should give the report title, date of the report, name and job title of the preparer, possibly the preparer's company name and address, and the name, job title, and possibly the company name and address of the person for whom the report is prepared. Although the amount and position of the title-page information may vary from one report to another, refer to the **Model Title Page** for an acceptable layout.

Letter of transmittal: a cover letter. When the transmittal letter is part of the pages of the report, it is placed immediately after the title page. Usually, it is a one-page letter on company letterhead that is addressed to the person for whom the report is prepared. It identifies the report by title, explains the purpose of it, and mentions important features, persons who may have helped prepare it, and any other relevant facts, particularly information that is not found in the text (body) of the report. It often concludes with an offer to answer questions or provide further information. (Some reports also include the letter of authorization that the preparer received; it then is placed immediately after the transmittal letter. Occasionally, a foreword written by an outside advocate is included in the report; it is placed immediately after the transmittal and authorization letters.)

Table of contents: an outline, with associated page numbers, of the main sections in the report. The contents page usually lists the headings and subheadings that are given throughout the report. Refer to the **Model Table of Contents** for a standard format. Notice that a long, formal report commonly follows the numbering of pages indicated in **PRINCIPAL PARTS OF A BOOK** in this chapter, with small roman numerals for the front-matter pages.

Lists of illustrations and tables: a page(s) prepared in a format similar to that of the contents page, listing the titles and captions of all tables and figures in the report, with associated page numbers. You may have one list for illustrations (photographs, charts, and diagrams) and another list for tables (straight tabular matter).

Abstract: a summary or synopsis of the report. It may be a condensed version of the information in the report, or it may discuss the objective of the report and what the report has accomplished. The length of an abstract or summary may vary from a few paragraphs to a hundred or more pages, depending on the size of the report. Even abstracts for small reports, however, must be fifty or more words. The style of abstracts and summaries varies greatly. Some are styled like the narrative in a book preface. Others use subheads, with numbered lists or one or more paragraphs after each subhead. The length and type of report and your office policy and style should guide you in the preparation of an abstract or summary.

Introduction: the statement of the problem that begins the body of the report. The first paragraph(s) in a report should briefly state what the subject of the report is, the purpose of the report, and what conclusions the report will present.

Background: a section following the introduction that provides information readers need to understand the main body of the report. The heading for this section may vary, depending on the subject and type of report, for example, Methodology, Review of Research, Company Policy, Scope of the Study, or History and Philosophy.

Data analysis: the main discussion of the problem. After the preliminary sections are presented, the theme of the report must be developed in a logical, step-by-step procedure. This part of the report may be broken down into numerous sections, each one introduced by a descriptive subhead. As the topic is discussed and arguments are logically put forth, additional supporting material should be referred to and positioned in the appropriate places in the manuscript. See **MANUSCRIPT-PREPARATION GUIDELINES** and other guidelines in this chapter for tips on preparing the various parts of a manuscript such as footnotes and tables.

Conclusions and recommendations: a statement of the results of the study and suggestions for a plan of action (if appropriate). This section, which immediately follows the main discussion, is often called Summary, Conclusions, Recommendations, or a combination such as Summary and Conclusions or Conclusions and Recommendations. Most concluding sections are brief reminders of the purpose of the report, its key points, the logical conclusions reached, and what should be done (recommendations) based upon the results of the study. The language should be persuasive (if appropriate), conclusive, and original; it should not merely repeat verbatim the earlier sentences and paragraphs.

Appendix: supporting material such as forms and tables. Supporting material that is not inserted within the text (body) of the report is collected in one or more appendixes following the conclusion or summary section. Usually, each appendix is given a number or letter (for example, Appendix A: Sample Questionnaires) and is prepared as a separate section of the manuscript. See also **MANUSCRIPT-PREPARATION GUIDELINES**, ILLUSTRATIONS, and **GUIDELINES FOR PREPARING TABLES** in this chapter.

Notes: a concluding section where text and other footnotes are collected. Although footnotes may be typed at the bottom of the appropriate text pages, they are often gathered in a single section after the appendix. See also **MANUSCRIPT-PREPARATION GUIDELINES,** NOTES AND BIBLIOGRAPHIES; **KINDS OF NOTES AND REFERENCE CITATIONS;** and **MODEL FOOTNOTES, BIBLIOGRAPHIES, AND CREDIT LINES** in this chapter.

Glossary: an alphabetical list of definitions of unfamiliar terms used in the report and other terms pertinent to the field of study. Although the glossary is commonly a separate section following the endnotes, it is sometimes treated as one of the appendixes (for example, Appendix E: Glossary). Refer to the Glossary in this book for an example of a common format.

Bibliography: resources cited and those used in preparing the report. This section, following the glossary, may also be called Works Cited or Works Consulted. The title Bibliography suggests a possible combination of works cited, consulted, and pertinent to the study. See **KINDS OF NOTES AND REFERENCE CITATIONS** and **MANUSCRIPT-PREPARATION GUIDELINES,** NOTES AND BIBLIOGRAPHIES, in this chapter.

Index: an alphabetical list of key subjects and terms in the report and page numbers where found. A book-length report may have an alphabetical index to names, places, and terms at the end of the report before the back cover (or final blank sheet if there is no cover). The listing may be brief and simple or detailed, with various levels of terms. See **INDEX-PREPARATION PROCEDURES** in this chapter for compilation guidelines and refer to the Index at the end of this book for an example of a common index format.

PROPOSALS

Some proposals are prepared in a business-report style as opposed to proposals for public and private grants, which usually must be prepared according to the strict specifications of the funding organization (sometimes using forms it provides). The informal business proposal may be presented in a brief letter or memo format or as a larger document. In both cases the writer must immediately catch the attention of the recipient in the opening paragraphs, must clearly and logically develop the proposal theme (and any request for funding), and must conclude with a forceful and persuasive summary and recommendations. Good documentation (statistics, tests, other reports, and so on) should be presented to back up the idea, product, or service being suggested, and the entire proposal package, including language and tone, must be businesslike but enthusiastic and persuasive.

Front matter: may consist of some or all items described in FORMAL REPORT: cover, flyleaf, title page, letter of transmittal, table of contents, lists of illustrations and tables, and abstract.

Body: may consist of some or all items described in FORMAL REPORT: introduction, background, data analysis, and conclusions and recommendations, with an additional section on the budget and an attached budget form, possibly prepared on a printed company form or one supplied by the funding organization.

End matter: may include appendixes with any supporting documents required to substantiate the basis of the proposal.

Model Title Page

COMPARISON OF MAJOR IRA PLANS

Prepared for
Janet F. McCarthy, General Manager
Benton Accounting Services, Inc.
300 North Main Street
Pittsburgh, Pennsylvania 15213

Prepared by
Donald Nagel, Consultant
Gemini Trust Management
1104 Lewis Avenue
Chicago, Illinois 60606

Model Table of Contents

CONTENTS

PRESS RELEASE CHARACTERISTICS

Principal Parts of Press Releases

SOURCE

Type the origin (person or organization) of the release, address, and telephone number at the top of the page in the upper-right corner. Some firms use printed press release stationery with the words "For further information call" positioned where the source data should be typed. See **Model Press Release.** After typing the source, leave several inches of blank space beneath it.

RELEASE DATE

A few inches below the source, type the date and the time that the material may be published by the recipients, for example, *FOR RELEASE TUESDAY, OCTOBER 6, 10 A.M.* Often this line is underscored and typed in all capitals. But unless it is absolutely necessary that the story be withheld until a specified time, simply say *FOR IMMEDIATE RELEASE.* See **Model Press Release.**

HEADLINE

Newspapers and magazines usually write the headlines (using the several inches of blank space that you leave following the source information). But some experienced public relations professionals supply their own headlines (to help editors determine the content at a glance) in all capitals a couple of lines above the release story.

DATELINE

Type the dateline—where and when the story occurred—two or more lines below the release date as the beginning words in the first paragraph. For example: *Chicago, June 5*. If the story occurred the same day you wrote the release, and you specified *FOR IMMEDIATE RELEASE*, the date of June 5 could be omitted. See **Model Press Release.**

BODY

Type the body of the release double-spaced, with paragraphs indented five to ten spaces. Begin with a brief (one sentence if possible) statement that answers the questions *who*, *what*, *where*, *when*, and *why*. This opening remark must also arouse the attention of the reader, for example: "Agreement was reached yesterday (*when*) on new safety measures (*what*) to prevent accidents (*why*) at Huntsville school crossings (*where*), according to Lewis Johnson, director of Huntsville Community Affairs (*who*)."

Following the lead, present the story in the order of most-important to least-important facts. This is necessary since editors usually condense stories to fit their available newspaper or magazine space by cutting off paragraphs from the bottom up. Keep the language factual and simple, using short, concise sentences. Avoid all colorful adjectives; for example, say "a new program," *not* "a *marvelous* new program." Edit your writing ruthlessly for simplicity, conciseness, and factual content, and double-check all facts for accuracy. The more usable your story is, without needing a lot of rewriting at the newspaper or magazine, the better the chance that it will be accepted. Identify people (and places) carefully, for example, "James M. Jones, 143 West End Avenue, Chicago," *not* "Jim Jones of Chicago" (there may be many people named Jim Jones in Chicago).

ENDING

Conclude the release using the same concise, factual style as in the rest of the body, keeping in mind that the final paragraphs may be deleted by the receiving editor. End each page with the word *-more-* centered about one to two inches from the bottom of the page. End the final page with the symbol *-30-* or ### in the same position. See **Model Press Release.**

Model Press Release

For further information call:

Jane R. Smith, Director
League for Concerned Citizens
Bellevue, WA 98009
206-111-1155

FOR IMMEDIATE RELEASE

Bellevue, Wash.—Bellevue will have a new community health center in 1986 to replace the one destroyed by fire earlier this year, according to center president Raymond E. Masterson. Plans for the new center were unveiled at the June 14 open board meeting.

The proposed construction at first was enthusiastically endorsed by the 123 community residents who attended the June meeting. But several citizens voiced their concern about the means of funding the project. Masterson admitted that contributions alone would not begin to pay for the new center. He then outlined a proposed increase in membership fees for all ages except those over seventy.

-more-

RESUME FORMATS

Professional-Achievement Format

JOB TITLE

(Identify the position you want.)

Name
Street
City/State/Zip Code
Telephone

OBJECTIVE

(Write a one-paragraph summary of the type of position
and geographic location desired and your willingness
to travel and relocate.)

EMPLOYMENT (OR EDUCATIONAL) HIGHLIGHTS

(Write a few paragraphs summarizing your current job
duties/responsibilities and achievements, type of
experience you have, significant duties undertaken,
positions previously held, and demonstrated strengths
and abilities in present and past positions. Summarize
the type of study program you pursued, special projects,
academic honors and achievements, and any work-study
activity.)

EMPLOYMENT

19XX-Present (State your title, company, city and state,
               type of firm, and brief summary of your
               responsibilities, with emphasis on any spe-
               cial job requirements, related expertise,
               personal initiative, and outstanding
               achievements.)

19XX–19XX   (Same data.)

EDUCATION

19XX–19XX   (State your school; city and state; degree or certificate of completion; summary of program, courses, or type of study, with emphasis on any academic honors and achievements or noteworthy performance.)

19XX–19XX   (Same data.)

LICENSES

(State the type of license you have and any associated qualifications or restrictions, the authorizing agency, license number, and expiration date.)

MILITARY RECORD

19XX–19XX   (State your branch, rank, responsibilities, and tours of duty; if you were honorably discharged and if you are in the reserve; and any special recognition or honors.)

OTHER ACCOMPLISHMENTS (AND QUALIFICATIONS)

(Write a summary of your other abilities and achievements: special-project work, creative endeavors, awards received, fluency in other languages, and special skills and abilities.)

MEMBERSHIPS

(List the organizations and associated data such as offices held with dates.)

PERSONAL DATA

(State your age, marital status, children, height, weight, citizenship status, and state of health.)

SALARY DESIRED

(State that you will negotiate, or specify an amount if important.)

REFERENCES

(Indicate whether references will be furnished on request or at the interview.)

AVAILABILITY

(Give the date you can start work or "immediately.")

Chronological Format

JOB TITLE

(Identify the position you want.)

Name
Street
City/State/Zip Code
Telephone

OBJECTIVE

(Write a one-paragraph summary of the type of position
and geographic location desired and your willingness
to travel and relocate.)

EMPLOYMENT

19XX-Present (State your job title, company, city and state,
type of firm, and brief summary of your
responsibilities and accomplishments.)

19XX–19XX   (Same data.)

EDUCATION

19XX–19XX   (State your school; city and state; degree
or certificate of completion; summary of
program, courses, or type of study and any
academic honors or achievements.)

19XX–19XX   (Same data.)

LICENSES

(State the type of license you have and any associated qualifications or restrictions, the authorizing agency, license
number, and expiration date.)

MILITARY RECORD

19XX–19XX   (State your branch, rank, responsibilities,
            and tours of duty; if you were honorably
            discharged and if you are in the reserve;
            and any special recognition or honors.)

OTHER ACCOMPLISHMENTS (AND QUALIFICATIONS)

(Write a summary of your other abilities and achievements; special-project work, creative endeavors, awards
received, fluency in other languages, and special skills and
abilities.)

MEMBERSHIPS

(List the organizations and associated data such as offices held with dates.)

PERSONAL DATA

(State your age, marital status, children, height, weight,
citizenship status, and state of health.)

SALARY DESIRED

(Indicate salary desired or whether you will negotiate.)

REFERENCES

(Indicate whether references will be furnished on request
or at the interview.)

AVAILABILITY

(Give the date you can start work or "immediately.")

PRINCIPAL PARTS OF A BOOK

FRONT MATTER

Half title (page i)
Series title, list of contributors, frontispiece, or blank (page ii)
Title page (page iii)
Copyright page (page iv)
Dedication or epigraph (page v)
Blank (page vi)
Table of contents (page vii)
List of illustrations (recto page)
List of tables (recto page)
Foreword (recto page)
Preface (recto page)
Acknowledgments, when not part of preface (recto page)
Introduction, when not part of body (recto page)

TEXT

Half title page, if any (recto page)
Part title page, if any (recto page)
First text page (recto page)

BACK MATTER

Appendixes (recto page)
Notes (recto page)
Glossary (recto page)
Bibliography (recto page)
Index (recto page)

NOTE: Recto = right-hand page.

CHART OF
PROOFREADER MARKS

In Margin	In Text	Meaning
e	letters	Delete.
	letters	Delete and close up.
stet.	writing reports	Let it stand.
	chapters	
no #	Examples show	No paragraph.
#	editingand	Add space.
out, sc	national of the	Something missing; see copy
sp. out	(4) people	Spell out.
	information	Close up.
	the division	Move left.
	the division	Move right.
tr	inductive	Transpose.
‖	tell the	
	client and	Line up, or align.
	editing. However	New paragraph.
?	1986	Question to author.
?	Is it true	Insert question mark.
!	Great	Insert exclamation mark.
=	non=American	Insert hyphen.
	as she said, Today	Insert quotation marks.
	revision however	Insert semicolon.
	the following copy	Insert colon.
	blue, red and green	Insert comma.
⊙	this report	Insert period.
	the readers viewpoint	Insert apostrophe.
b	look	Change to b.

In Margin	In Text	Meaning
caps (or ≡)	<u>Summary</u>	Set in capital letters.
lc	PREFACE	Set in lowercase letters.
bf (or ◠◠)	Writing and Editing	Set in boldface type.
ital (or —)	<u>Writing Handbook</u>	Set in italic type.
S.C. (or =)	<u>a.m.</u> or <u>p.m.</u>	Set in small capital letters.
C. + S.C.	<u>Editing Guide</u>	Set in caps and small caps.
✓✓✓	k✓e✓y✓topics	Correct spacing.
▭	▭ Open the discussion	Indent one em.
(*rom.*)	*Introduction*	Change to roman type.
⌄3/	footnote∨3	Set as superior number.
∧1	B∧R	Set as inferior number.
[/]	∧a + b∧	Insert brackets.
(/)	∧a + b∧	Insert parentheses.
—/M	and chapters—M these	one-em dash.

NOTE: See also **SAMPLE PAGE OF EDITED AND TYPEMARKED MANUSCRIPT, PROOFREADING GALLEYS AND PAGE PROOFS,** and **SAMPLE MARKED PAGE PROOF** in this chapter.

SAMPLE PAGES OF EDITED AND TYPEMARKED MANUSCRIPT

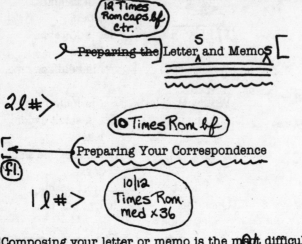

12 Times Rom caps bf ctr.

Preparing the Letter and Memos

2l # >

10 Times Rom bf

fl.

Preparing Your Correspondence

1 l # >   *10/12 Times Rom. med x36*

Composing your letter or memo is the most difficult part

correspondence   may be   a that
of preparing business writing. Maybe it's the only prt

s   your   will
concerning you. But readers notice more. In most types

business   appearances
of writing, the way things look is matters a great deal.

Your message   and memos
What you say may be brilliant but if your letters don't use

elements   your   will not
and position the principal parts properly readers won't

favorably   skill   a
be impressed with you as a communicator. Ech of the stan-

ar   and memos   below alphabetically Examples of
dard pts of letters is described here. Sample of the parts

many of these elements appear in   illustrated
are shown in the formats shown on pages 122-123.

Attention line

When a letter is addressed to a company, you may direct it to a particular departments or person by using an attention line. (Attention: Data Processing Department; Attention William Smith).

If that person is absent, someone else in the company or department will handle the matter. The attention line is positioned directly beneath the inside address. Each major word is capitalized, but the trend is away from underscoring.

Body

The body of a letter usually starts after the salutation or subject line. In the simplified format, the body begins after the subject.

NOTE: Circled instructions are the type specifications to be followed by the typesetter. For example, 10/12 Times Rom. med. X36 means 10-point type leaded (space between lines) 2 points in a medium (as opposed to light or dark) style of type called Times Roman to be set in a page column that is 36 picas wide. The common formula is 12 points = 1 pica and 6 picas = 1 inch. See **PICAS AND EQUIVALENT INCHES** in Chapter 5 and **CHART OF PROOFREADER MARKS** in this chapter.

EDITING CHECKLIST

FORMAT

Format follows publisher/employer requirements. ( )

Format is appropriate for topic and type of project. ( )

Format is applied consistently throughout manuscript. ( )

Manuscript is prepared in a regular type face, not script, italic, or bold. ( )

Manuscript is double-spaced, including notes, tables, and other supporting material, with adequate margins. ( )

FRONT MATTER

Preliminary pages are complete and in proper order:
Title/half-title page(s) ( )
Copyright page ( )
Dedication/epigraph page ( )

Table of contents ( )
List of illustrations ( )
List of tables ( )
Foreword ( )
Preface ( )
Acknowledgments ( )
Introduction ( )

BACK MATTER

End matter is complete and in proper order:
Appendixes ( )
Notes ( )
Reference list ( )
Glossary ( )
Bibliography ( )

ILLUSTRATIONS

Illustrations are complete and in proper order. ( )

Each piece is essential to enhance the text discussion, not merely cosmetic. ( )

Reference is made to each piece in the text discussion. ( )

Figure numbers and captions have been cross-checked with the references to each piece in the text discussion for accuracy, consistency, and proper sequence. ( )

Original artwork is collected apart from the text manuscript pages. ( )

Figure captions have been cross-checked with titles on the list of illustrations in the front matter for consistency. ( )

Permission has been secured from copyright owners for reprint material.   ( )

TABLES

Tables are complete and in proper order.   ( )

Proper table format is used.   ( )

Reference is made to each table in the text discussion.   ( )

Table numbers and titles have been cross-checked with the references to each piece in the text discussion for accuracy, consistency, and proper sequence.   ( )

Numerous large tables are collected apart from the text discussion pages or are grouped at the ends of chapters or at the end of the manuscript.   ( )

Table titles have been cross-checked with titles on the list of tables in the front matter for consistency.   ( )

Permission has been secured from copyright owners for reprint material.   ( )

REFERENCES

Notes and other references are complete and in proper order.   ( )

Notes are typed at the foot of appropriate text pages or in a notes section after the appendixes.   ( )

Reference lists are typed alphabetically after the endnotes section.   ( )

Bibliography entries are typed alphabetically at the end of the manuscript just before the index.   ( )

Note numbers have been cross-checked with corresponding numbers in the text discussion for accuracy and consistency. ( )

Footnote facts have been cross-checked with reference-list and bibliography entries for accuracy and consistency. ( )

Reference-list entries have been cross-checked with in-text citation facts for accuracy and consistency. ( )

Bibliography entries have been cross-checked with notes and reference-list facts for accuracy and consistency. ( )

QUOTATIONS

Quoted material is copied verbatim from its source, with *sic* in brackets after errors that appeared in the original. ( )

Ellipsis points (periods) are used to designate omitted words or passages. ( )

Quoted material is typed as an indented block of copy (*extract*) when it is eight or more lines long. ( )

Quoted material is used with the permission of the copyright owner when the total number of quoted words exceeds the limit indicated by your publisher or employer. ( )

TITLES

Concise, descriptive statements are used. ( )

Parallel (similar style of expression) heads are used. ( )

Correct punctuation and grammar are used.   ( )

Heads and titles are capitalized correctly and
consistently.   ( )

Different levels of heads in the manuscript are
easily distinguished.   ( )

Titles and heads have been cross-checked with the
table of contents for consistency.   ( )

OPENING

The opening passage hooks readers immediately.   ( )

Opening remarks are clearly related to the text
discussion and introduce readers to the topic of
the text.   ( )

The opening is brief and moves readers immediately into the body of the text.   ( )

The opening has a smooth transition to the body
of the text.   ( )

ENDING

The concluding passage draws the text discussion
to a prompt and logical conclusion.   ( )

The ending reinforces essential points of the text
discussion.   ( )

Final remarks do not leave readers confused or
with unanswered questions.   ( )

The ending leaves readers with the desired
impression.   ( )

SECTIONS

Information is organized into logical sections.   ( )

Sections are in appropriate sequence to develop
the thesis or theme clearly and logically.   ( )

Brief, descriptive headings are used to identify the
sections.   ( )

Sections have smooth transitions from one to
another.   ( )

SENTENCES

Sentences use correct syntax and grammar.   ( )

Sentences use the active voice as much as possible.   ( )

Sentences make short, concise statements when-
ever possible.   ( )

Transitions from one sentence to another are smooth
and clear.   ( )

PARAGRAPHS

Paragraphs consist of sentences combined properly
to form well-developed, easy-to-read units.   ( )

Each one has an effective lead (topic) sentence.   ( )

Each one has a concluding sentence that moves
the discussion smoothly to the next paragraph.   ( )

Lengthy, cumbersome passages are divided into
two or more smaller paragraphs.   ( )

SPELLING

Manuscript has been read for typographical errors.   ( )

Manuscript has been examined for commonly mis-spelled words.   ( )

Words with acceptable spelling variations are used consistently.   ( )

Prefixes and suffixes are spelled correctly and used consistently.   ( )

Numbers are used consistently as figures or words.   ( )

Abbreviations in nontechnical material are gener-ally avoided.   ( )

GRAMMAR

Parts of speech are used correctly.   ( )

Proper subject-verb agreement is used.   ( )

Clauses such as restrictive and nonrestrictive clauses are used and punctuated properly.   ( )

Manuscript has been checked for overall grammati-cal accuracy.   ( )

PUNCTUATION

Manuscript has been read for typographical errors and misplaced punctuation.   ( )

Consistent punctuation style is used.   ( )

Prefixes, compounds, and other forms are punctu-ated consistently and accurately.   ( )

Highly visible punctuation such as the dash and
exclamation point is not overused.   ( )

Underscoring (for emphasis) is used sparingly.   ( )

Words are divided properly at the ends of lines,
with end-of-line hyphens in no more than two
succeeding lines.   ( )

CAPITALIZATION

Publisher/employer preferred style is used.   ( )

Selected style-book pattern is used consistently.   ( )

Chosen capitalization style is used consistently.   ( )

Manuscript does not use excessive capitalization
of familiar terms.   ( )

WORD CHOICE

Appropriate language for the topic and project is
used.   ( )

Effective and persuasive language is used.   ( )

Words with a precise meaning are used.   ( )

Short, familiar words are generally used instead of
long, unfamiliar words.   ( )

Incorrect and weak language has been deleted or
changed.   ( )

Manuscript has been reviewed for commonly misused words.   ( )

CLARITY

Discussion is well organized and easy to follow.   ( )

Text has a logical progression of points.   ( )

Complex concepts are amplified or simplified.   ( )

Sentences and paragraphs are generally short and
easy to read.   ( )

Statements are accurate and responsible.   ( )

Vague and misleading expressions have been deleted or changed.   ( )

Facts have been verified and adequately explained.   ( )

CONCISENESS

Nonessential material has been deleted.   ( )

Rambling and wordiness have been deleted.   ( )

Redundancy has been deleted.   ( )

Unnecessary introductions and summaries have been
deleted.   ( )

CLICHES

Cliches, irrelevancies, and other trite expressions
have been deleted or changed.   ( )

POMPOSITY

Pomposity, vogue words, and euphemisms have
been deleted or changed.   ( )

JARGON

Jargon and gobbledygook have been deleted or
changed.   ( )

BIAS

Discriminatory expressions have been deleted or
changed.   ( )

OTHER   ( )

NOTE: Most manuscripts need careful editing, even those of
professional writers; often the editing involves several read-
ings of the manuscript. To use this checklist to edit your own
work (and as a reminder of the many facets of good writing),
put an asterisk by categories that apply to your manuscript
(for example, your project may have illustrations but no
tables). Then select a few similar items from the list and
review your manuscript with only those items in mind (trying
to check too many things at one time can be confusing). Next
select a few more similar items and check the manuscript
again. Continue this procedure until every pertinent category
on the checklist has been covered and you are satisfied that
no further corrections are needed.

PROOFREADING GALLEYS
AND PAGE PROOFS

GALLEY PROOFS

Galleys, or *galley proofs,* are sheets of typeset material,
without illustrations, running heads, and final page breaks.
The name *galley* comes from the use of a shallow metal tray

into which type is deposited from a typesetting machine (see **BASIC TYPESETTING PROCESSES,** LINOTYPE and MONO-TYPE, in this chapter). Galley proofs are provided by type-setters for customers to use in proofreading their typeset material and making corrections before the set copy is divided into final pages. They are also provided for use as rough typeset copy that can be cut apart and pasted onto page-size sheets in preparing a page-by-page layout (*dummy*) of the proposed publication. Changes made by a customer, such as rewriting, are less costly at the galley stage than at the page-proof or a later stage, but rewriting and revision should be done on the manuscript, *before* the copy is submitted to the typesetter.

PAGE PROOFS

Page proofs are sheets of typeset text material divided into actual pages, with running heads, page numbers, footnotes, and so on in the proper position and with boxes drawn or blank spaces left where illustrations are to appear. Some manuscript copy is set directly in pages, skipping the galley stage. But when galleys are provided, they are proofread first, and galley errors are corrected before the set copy is divided into pages.

Reproduction proofs, or *repros*, are corrected page proofs prepared on a white, coated paper suitable for photographing. Rewriting and revision at this point is expensive and should be avoided. Such alterations are even more costly at the stage of *negative proofs* (or *press proofs*). At this stage the final text and illustrations are printed on a proof of sensitized paper that may cause the material to appear blue (*blueprint*) or some other color. All of the proofs—galleys, pages, repros, and negative/press proofs—are prepared so that customers can proofread copy and check material for completeness and position *before* the final product is printed.

READING COPY

Some proofreading is handled by two persons—one reading from the original manuscript and the other one following and marking corrections on the sheets of proof. Most proofreading, however, is handled by one person who glances back and forth from manuscript to proof. Proofreading must be done word by word and line by word, with attention to every detail.

CHECKING FOR ERRORS

During the first proofreading session, all spelling, punctuation, grammatical, and other errors should be marked on the sheets of proof in the margins, left or right, nearest the error, using carets and other marks within the text to show where the margin corrections should be made. See **SAMPLE MARKED PAGE PROOF** in this chapter for an illustration of a properly marked galley or page proof. In addition to checking for misplaced punctuation, misspellings, and so on, watch for correct and consistent spacing in lists and extracts, as well as paragraph indentation, position of subheads, and use of the correct typeface for each element of the manuscript.

MARKING CORRECTIONS

Separate corrections to be made on the same line of type with a slash, for example, h/lc (lc = lowercase). Place the corrections in the order, left to right, that they are to be made in the line of text. In the case of h/lc, the correction of the letter *h* comes first in the line, followed by the "lowercase" instruction. See the examples in **SAMPLE MARKED PAGE PROOF.** When the same correction is to be made more than once in the same line of text, with no intervening corrections, write it once in the margin followed by a slant line for each succeeding occurrence (for example, h// means that the correction is to be made twice in the adjacent line of text).

ADDING MATERIAL

To add material, put a caret in the text where you want the new copy to go and write what you want to be inserted in the galley- or page-proofs margin or on a separate sheet of paper if it is too long to fit on the proof. If you use a separate sheet, write in the proof margin "insert A [or whatever you label it] here" and then label the separate sheet "A" and write "insert A on galley [or page] number _____." In the margin of the proof circle the initials *aa* (author's alteration) when you make a change that is *your* new addition or correction rather than correction of an error made by the typesetter.

DELETING MATERIAL

To delete material, cross it out and place a delete sign in the margin. For examples of the proper symbols to use in marking such corrections, see **CHART OF PROOFREADER MARKS** in this chapter. If you change your mind after deleting something, put a row of dots beneath each line of crossed-out text and write "stet" (let it stand) in the margin. To delete old and substitute new material, cross out the old and simply write the new in the margin (or on a separate sheet of paper).

CHECKING GALLEYS

After you proofread galley proofs and mark all errors and new revisions, the typesetter will make the corrections and changes. Usually, you will then be given page proofs that show the completed corrections and changes. Compare the galley proofs on which you marked the errors and changes against the new page proofs. Check to see if each correction and change that you marked on the galleys has been made. If the typesetter overlooked something, mark it again on the page proofs the same as you did on the galley proofs. Follow the same procedure when you check page proofs against reproduction proofs or reproduction proofs against press proofs. Keep marking corrections and changes that the typesetter forgets to make (or that *you* forgot to mark previously) on each new set of proofs until everything is complete and correct.

CHECKING PAGES

After you check galleys against pages to see whether all corrections were made, you need to examine the pages for accuracy and position of running heads and page numbers. Also check facing (side-by-side) pages to be certain that they are the same length and that paragraphs are in proper sequence. Look whether illustrations and captions, footnotes, titles, and other material are in the right place on each page. Mark *widows* (short lines falling at the top of a page) and other undesirable page breaks. Generally, examine each page for appearance as well as errors.

INDEXING

If your material is to have an index, ask for an extra set of page proofs (which have page numbers) so that you can underline key terms on each page. For further guidelines see **INDEX-PREPARATION PROCEDURES** in this chapter.

RELEASING COPY

When you are satisfied that the final proof you see is correct and complete, mark it "ok" and return it to the typesetter or printer, keeping in mind that once the material goes to press, no further changes or corrections are possible.

INDEX-PREPARATION PROCEDURES

MARKING PAGE PROOFS

A common procedure in preparing an index, particularly for an inexperienced indexer, is first to go through a full set of page proofs and on each page underline all words that you want to have in the index and write in the margins all general subjects that you want to include. You do not have to make final decisions at this time about which words will be main entries (main headings in the index), subentries (subheadings), or sub-subentries (sub-subheadings). Some indexers, however, edit directly on the page proofs while underlining.

You might, for example, underline the words *manuscript* and *preparation* in a paragraph about writing. You might then decide on the spot that *manuscript* should be a main entry and *preparation* a subentry. To distinguish between the two levels, some indexers use a symbol such as a checkmark or colon *after* a main entry and *before* a subentry. You might also decide to jot the word *of* after *preparation* on the page proof to further designate it as a modifier of *manuscript*.

ENTERING TERMS ON CARDS

When you have done all of the underlining and editing that you want to do on the page proofs, write *each* word, phrase,

SAMPLE MARKED PAGE PROOF

HOW TO CORRECT PROOF

It does not appear that the earliest printers had any method of correcting errors before the form was on the press. The learned correctors of the first two centuries of printing were not proofreaders in our sense; they were rather what we should term office editors. Their labors were chiefly to see that the proof corresponded to the copy, but that the printed page was correct in its latinity, that the words were there, and that the sense was right. They cared but little about orthography, bad letters, or purely printers' errors, and when the text seemed to them wrong they consulted fresh authorities or altered it on their own responsibility. Good proofs, in the modern sense, were impossible until professional readers were employed, men who had first a printer's education, and then spent many years in the correction of proof. The orthography of English, which for the past century has undergone little change, was very fluctuating until after the publication of Johnson's Dictionary, and capitals, which have been used with considerable regularity for the past 80 years, were previously used on the miss or hit plan. The approach to regularity, so far as we have, may be attributed to the growth of a class of professional proofreaders, and it is to them that we owe the correctness of modern printing. More errors have been found in the Bible than in any other one work. For many generations it was frequently the case that Bibles were brought out stealthily, from fear of governmental interference. They were frequently printed from imperfect texts, and were often modified to meet the views of those who published them. The story is related that a certain woman in Germany, who was the wife of a printer, and had become disgusted with the continual assertion of the superiority of man over woman which she had heard, hurried into the composing room while her husband was at supper and altered a sentence in the Bible, which he was printing, so that it read, Narr, instead of Herr, thus making the verse read "And he shall be thy fool" instead of "And he shall be thy lord." The word not was omitted by Barker, the King's printer in England in 1632, in printing the seventh commandment. He was fined £3,000 on this account.

Source: From *Private Secretary's Encyclopedic Dictionary*, 3d ed., revised by Mary A. De Vries. © 1984 by Prentice-Hall, Inc. Published by Prentice-Hall, Inc., Englewood Cliffs, N.J. 07632.

or subject, with the page number where it appears, on *a separate index card* (usually three by five inches). The cards with words you already labeled on the page proofs as subentries should list the main entry followed by the subentry and the corresponding page number. (Some indexes use section numbers, chapter numbers, or other locator numbers in place of or in addition to the page numbers.)

Since *each* term, whether a main entry or subentry, goes on a *separate* card, you may have many cards all beginning with the same main entry (for example, *manuscript*), but each card will have a different subentry. Double-check the corresponding page number after you type each card, and for now, keep the cards in the order typed so that you can more easily locate the same information on the page proofs.

Example: Manuscript
                  - preparation of, 72

                  Manuscript
                  - writing of, 134

                  Manuscript
                  - editing of, 13

                  Manuscript
                  - typing of, 114

ALPHABETIZING THE CARDS

After you have typed a card for each word(s) and subject and checked each one against the page proofs for accuracy, put all of the cards in alphabetical groups, A to Z. For example, all cards beginning with the word *manuscript* would go into the group of M's. Next alphabetize the main entries within each letter of the alphabet. For example, *manuscript, markup, matrix,* and *mechanical* might be main entries in the M section. Then alphabetize all of the cards having the same main entry by subentry and after that by sub-subentry.

Example: Manuscript
                  editing of, 13

Manuscript
- preparation of, 72

Manuscript
- typing of, 114

Manuscript
- writing of, 134

EDITING THE CARDS

After all of the cards are in alphabetical order by main entry and then by subentry and sub-subentry, cross out the same main entry in front of successive subentries and combine all references to the same main entry on one card, again double-checking spelling and page numbers for accuracy. You may discover several cards with the same main entry and even several with the same subentry but with different page numbers. Use inclusive numbers, where appropriate.

Example: Manuscript
- editing of, 13, 24

~~Manuscript~~
- preparation of, 72–73

~~Manuscript~~
- typing of, 114, 123–24

~~Manuscript~~
- writing of, 134, 200–205, 307–8

While editing, be certain that you have distinguished sub-subentries from subentries and main entries. Capitalize the first word and any proper noun in the main entry. Lowercase the first word of subentries and sub-subentries.

Example: Manuscript
- typing of, 114, 123–24
-- computer, 115
-- typewriter, 123–24
-- word processor, 115–16

Make final adjustments in wording (check for grammatical and spelling accuracy) and change main entries to subentries or vice versa as needed. Add cross-references in appropriate places.

Example: Manuscript. <u>See also</u> Copy.
- typing of, 114, 123–24
-- computer, 115
-- typewriter, 123–24
-- word processor, 115–16

TYPING THE INDEX

Type the index, double-spaced, on twenty-pound white bond paper, 8½ by 11 inches, in one column. Leave extra space between each section of the alphabet and number the pages, beginning with 1. Delete the hyphens or other symbols that you used to distinguish subentries from sub-subentries while editing. When typing an index in list style, indent subentries three to four character spaces. Refer to the index in this book for an example of the list format. If your index has main entries and subentries but no sub-subentries, you may be able to use a run-in style.

Example: Manuscript: editing of, 13, 24; preparation of, 72–73; typing of, 114, 123–24; writing of, 134, 200–205, 307–8

PROOFREADING

Proofread the typed index manuscript against the edited index cards. Correct all errors and make any final adjustments and revisions *before* you submit the index to the typesetter.

BASIC TYPESETTING PROCESSES

TYPEWRITER AND WORD PROCESSOR/COMPUTER

Often called *cold type*, typewriter and word-processor/computer composition refers to the preparation of copy by one of the various typewriters (manual, electric, electronic, magnetic tape) or by word processors/computers. Although material typed by most manual and electric typewriters cannot be justified (that is, have a straight right margin), more advanced machines (for example, electronic and magnetic-tape Selectric) and word processors/computers have proportional spacing and can create a straight right margin. Copy prepared on paper by typewriter or word processor/computer can be photographed directly and an offset printing plate prepared from the negatives. Simple typewriter or word-processor/computer composition is generally less expensive than the other composition methods, but depending on the equipment, the quality of the prepared images may be lower.

PHOTOCOMPOSITION

Modern photocomposition machines have replaced many of the earlier photo-based typesetters. The newest machines are electronically controlled. These modern electronic machines have a keyboard for preparing the copy; information is stored in digital form, and images are shown on video screens. The images are then transmitted to paper or film; an offset negative can be prepared from the final corrected copy and an offset printing plate made from the negative. This typesetting process is often loosely referred to as *cold type*, like the typewriter method, since no cast metal is involved as it is in the hot-type methods such as Linotype and Monotype.

LINOTYPE

Often called *hot type*, the Linotype method of composition uses a keyboard to produce solid lines of type. Each line of type is cast in a molten type metal, forming a slug that is dropped into a galley (tray). Linotype composition is usually less expensive than Monotype, except that a correction with this method involves resetting and replacing the entire line. Copy for proofreading is usually first presented in long galley sheets, followed by page proofs. After final corrections are made, the pages are ready for printing.

MONOTYPE

Also called *hot type*, the Monotype process uses a keyboard to prepare a punched tape that is run on a casting machine. This machine casts single letters of type and then assembles them into lines in a galley (tray). Unlike corrections with Linotype, a correction with Monotype does not involve resetting the entire line. As in the case of Linotype composition, though, copy here is also usually presented first in long galley sheets, followed by page proofs. After final corrections are made, the pages are ready for printing.

NOTE: See **BASIC PRINTING PROCESSES** in this chapter for information on the processes by which typeset material is printed. See also **PROOFREADING GALLEYS AND PAGE PROOFS** in this chapter.

BASIC PRINTING PROCESSES

OFFSET

A popular and common process, offset lithography involves, first, the preparation of reproduction proofs (repros),
a special paper proof, from the typeset material; next, the
preparation of a photograph negative of the repro; and finally,
the preparation of an offset plate from the negative, which
will be used to make the inked impression on paper. The
offset process can be used for a great variety of printing
needs. Ordinary typed copy can be photographed and printed
by this means too. Quality varies depending on the press and
the quality of the copy and the resultant photograph from
which the plate is made.

LETTERPRESS

The letterpress process is the oldest process but is less
common today than offset lithography. Letterpress printing is
based upon a relief principle, using, for example, type, pho-
toengravings, and wood or linoleum cuts to produce the
printed material. Raised surfaces are inked and then pressed
against the paper to make an impression. Letterpress printing
is done on rotary, vertical, and cylinder presses. It can be
used for newspapers, magazines, books, and a variety of
other material.

GRAVURE

The gravure process is based upon the intaglio principle.
This means that the lines to be printed are cut below the
surface of the plate, and the ink is wiped off the plate surface
but left in the depressions that will be printed on the paper.

Gravure work is done on a rotary press. It is noted for its use in color reproduction and for speciality work such as label printing.

NOTE: See **BASIC TYPESETTING PROCESSES** in this chapter for a description of the methods used to prepare material for printing.

COPYRIGHTING

COPYRIGHT ACT OF 1976

According to Title 17 of the United States Code, effective January 1, 1978, all published and unpublished works that are fixed in a copy or phonorecord are subject to a single system of statutory protection. The copyright owner has the exclusive right to reproduce an original work and to prepare derivative works. Although registration of a work in the Library of Congress Copyright Office is not necessary to have a valid copyright, it is necessary for bringing a court action in regard to infringement.

WORKS COPYRIGHTED BEFORE 1978

The maximum total term of copyright protection for works already protected by federal statute is now seventy-five years: a first term of twenty-eight years from the date of the original copyright plus a renewal term of forty-seven years (instead of an additional twenty-eight years as previously allowed). Application for renewal must be made within one year before the first twenty-eight-year term expires. Copyrights already renewed that were in their second term between December 31,

1976, and December 31, 1977, have been automatically extended to last the full seventy-five years. Ask the Copyright Office for Circular R15 and renewal From RE.

WORKS COPYRIGHTED JANUARY 1, 1978, AND AFTER

The new law, which establishes a single copyright term with no renewal requirements, applies to works created on or after January 1, 1978. Works existing on January 1, 1978, but not copyrighted and not in the public domain are subject to automatic federal copyright protection.

The term of protection under the new law is a basic life-plus-fifty-years system (in effect in most other countries). Copyright protection therefore applies for the life of the author(s) plus fifty years after the death of the last surviving author. For works made for hire and anonymous or pseudonymous works, the protection applies for seventy-five years from publication or one hundred years from creation, whichever is shorter.

YEAR-END-EXPIRATION RULE

All copyright terms will run through the end (December 31) of the calendar year in which they would otherwise expire. The renewal period for works originally copyrighted between 1950 and 1977 will run from December 31 of the twenty-seventh year of the copyright until December 31 of the following year.

WORKS IN THE PUBLIC DOMAIN

Works in the public domain are not protected under the new law; also, copyright that has been lost on a work cannot be restored. Works can fall into the public domain if they do not meet requirements such as containing the proper copyright notice or if their terms of protection have expired.

FAIR USE

The 1976 copyright law gives four criteria to use in determining whether copying material from a particular source without permission or payment is fair:

1. The purpose and character of the use, including whether such use is of a commercial nature or is for nonprofit educational purposes

2. The nature of the copyrighted work

3. The amount and substantiality of the portion used in relation to the copyrighted work as a whole

4. The effect of the use upon the potential market for, or value of, the copyrighted work

According to Section 107 of the 1976 law, "the fair use of a copyrighted work, including such use by reproduction in copies or phonorecords or by any other means specified by that section, for purposes such as criticism, comment, news reporting, teaching (including multiple copies for classroom use), scholarship, or research, is not an infringement of copyright." Although the 1976 law does not include guidelines for classroom copying, systematic reproduction and distribution of single or multiple copies of books and periodicals by libraries (instead of their purchase) is forbidden. Under sets of guidelines developed separately by author, educator, and publisher representatives, spontaneous copying for classroom use must not exceed the number of students in a course, each copy must bear a copyright notice, and the amount copied must be brief. For a detailed review of fair use, consult the text of the 1976 law or a current copyright handbook.

COPYRIGHT NOTICE

A proper notice of copyright must be published in a printed work. It must include the letter *c* in a circle (and may also include the word *copyright,* or the abbreviation *copr.*), the year of first publication of the work, and the name of the copyright owner, for example, *Copyright © 1986 by New American Library.* A U.S. citizen whose work includes a proper copyright notice also receives protection in all other countries that are members of the Universal Copyright Convention.

INFORMATION AND FORMS

Write to the Copyright Office, Library of Congress, Washington, D.C. 20559, for free forms and ask for instructions on the proper procedure for registering a work and the applicable fee to submit. Since different forms are used for different types of works, indicate what type of work you want to protect. For a general discussion of the 1976 act, consult a current handbook such as Donald F. Johnson's *Copyright Handbook* (New York: R. R. Bowker, 1978), which also provides the text of the copyright acts of 1909 and 1976 and contains sample registration forms and fair-use and reproduction guidelines.

5. REFERENCE SECTION

Professional writers as well as beginners need a wide range of facts and figures to help them prepare their messages. Information sources, lists of abbreviations, postal regulations, and various statistical data are only a few examples of the technical material that writers draw upon to conduct research, write and edit their copy, type or typeset communications and publications, and send what they have prepared. Although most of us take such basic material for granted, our bookshelves are lined with reference works. Those who write know that without this material close at hand, a writer's work is inevitably complicated; with it readily available, however, the job is made much easier.

RELEASE FORMS

Model Release

TO:_____

_____

_____

I hereby give _____ the absolute right and permission to copyright and/or publish and/or resell photographic portraits or pictures of me, or in which I may be included in whole or in part, for art, advertising, trade, or any other lawful purpose whatsoever.

I hereby waive any right that I may have to inspect and/or approve the finished product or the advertising copy that may be used in connection therewith or the use to which it may be applied.

I hereby release, discharge, and agree to save _____ _____ from any liability by virtue of any blurring, distortion, alteration, optical illusion, or use in composite form, whether intentional or otherwise, that may occur or be produced in the making of said pictures or in any processing tending toward the completion of the finished product.

Date_____   Model_____

Guardian_____   Address_____

Witness_____   _____

Photographic Release

Dear _____.

May we please have permission to reproduce the photograph(s) indicated below for inclusion in _____ _____ and for any and all revisions, adaptations, and subsidiary and/or derivative rights, uses, or works of the Work and for all commercial and trade purposes in perpetuity throughout the world.

In signing this permission, you warrant and agree to hold us harmless that you are the absolute owner of the photograph(s) and the use contemplated by this permission will not infringe upon the copyright or any other right of third parties.

Sincerely,

_____

MATERIAL TO REPRODUCED:_____
_____
_____
_____
_____

Permission is granted by: _____ Date: _____

Form of Copyright Acknowledgment:_____
_____
_____
_____

Interview Release

TO:

_____

_____

_____

I, _____, have examined _____
_____
by _____ and affirm that I am
quoted accurately in the manuscript.

Date_____   Address_____

Signature_____   _____

NOTE: Advertising agencies, broadcasting companies, magazines, and other organizations usually have their own (often
detailed) release forms prepared by an attorney. Other organizations and individuals, such as freelance writers, may use a
standard form or prepare one of their own especially worded
to suit their needs.

BASIC LIBRARY
CLASSIFICATION SYSTEMS

Dewey Decimal System

000. General works
100. Philosophy
200. Religion
300. Sociology
400. Philology

500. Natural science
600. Useful arts
700. Fine arts
800. Literature
900. History

Library of Congress System

A.   General works and polygraphy
B.   Philosophy and religion
C.   History and auxiliary sciences
D.   History and topography outside the United States
E, F. American history and topography
G.   Geography and anthropology
H.   Social sciences
J.   Political sciences
K.   Law
L.   Education
M.   Music
N.   Fine arts
P.   Language and literature
Q.   Science
R.   Medicine
S.   Agriculture and plant and animal husbandry
T.   Technology
U.   Military science
V.   Naval science
Z.   Library science and bibliography

NOTE: The ten Dewey Decimal categories may be subdivided as needed (100, 110, 120; 120.1, 120.2, 120.3; and so on). The twenty Library of Congress categories may be combined as needed (HG, MN, and so on), with additional numbers and letters indicating further subdivisions of categories.

SELECTED REFERENCE SOURCES

ATLASES

Ambassador World Atlas (Hammond)
Goode's World Atlas (Rand McNally)
International World Atlas (Hammond)
North American Road Atlas (American Automobile Association)
Rand McNally Road Atlas (Rand McNally)

BUSINESS AND FINANCIAL PUBLICATIONS

Barron's, National Business Financial Weekly
Business Week
Commercial and Financial Chronicle (semiweekly)
The Conference Board Business Record (monthly)
Consumer Reports (monthly)
Current Industrial Reports (quarterly or throughout the year)
Dun & Bradstreet Reference Book (bimonthly)
Dun's Review and Modern Industry (monthly)
Economic Indicators (monthly)
Federal Reserve Bulletin (monthly)
Fortune (monthly)
Harvard Business Review (monthly)
Monthly Labor Review
Moody's Investors Service (for example, *Bond Record, Manual of Investments, Industrial Manual,* and *Handbook of Common Stocks*)
Nation's Business (monthly)
The New York Times (daily)
Prentice-Hall Federal Tax Guide (annual)

Standard and Poor's Corporation (for example, *Standard Corporation Records, Standard and Poor's Trade and Securities Service, Standard and Poor's Bond Guide*, and *The Outlook*)
Survey of Current Business (monthly)
Value Line (loose-leaf service)
Wall Street Journal (daily)

DATABASE UTILITIES

CompuServe Information Service
CompuServe
5000 Arlington Centre Boulevard
Columbus, OH 43220

DIALOG
Lockheed Information Systems
3460 Hillview Avenue
Palo Alto, CA 94304

Dow Jones News/Retrieval Service
Dow Jones & Co.
P.O. Box 300
South Brunswick, NJ 08540

The Information Bank-NYTIS
New York Times Information Service
Suite 86035
One World Trade Center
New York, NY 10048

LEXIS
Mead Data Central
200 Park Avenue
New York, NY 10016

SDC Search Service
System Development Corporation
2500 Colorado Avenue
Santa Monica, CA 90406

The Source
Source Telecomputing Corporation
1616 Anderson Road
McLean, VA 22102

DICTIONARIES, WORD BOOKS, AND QUOTATION SOURCES

Bartlett's Familiar Quotations (Little, Brown)
Black's Law Dictionary (West)
Dictionary of American Slang (Crowell)
Dictionary of Education (McGraw-Hill)
Dictionary of the Social Sciences (Free Press)
McGraw-Hill Dictionary of Scientific and Technical Terms (McGraw-Hill)
Oxford English Dictionary (Clarendon Press)
Roget's International Thesaurus (Harper & Row)
Stedman's Medical Dictionary (Scribner's)
Technical Terms (McGraw-Hill)
Webster's New World Thesaurus (Merriam)
Webster's Ninth New Collegiate Dictionary (Merriam)
Webster's Third New International Dictionary (Merriam)

DIRECTORIES

American Medical Directory (American Medical Association)
Congressional Record (U.S. Government Printing Office)
Current Bigraphy (Wilson)
Directory of Corporations, Directors, and Executives (Standard and Poor's Corp., McGraw-Hill)

Dun & Bradstreet Reference Book (Dun & Bradstreet)
The Federal Register (U.S. Government Printing Office)
Gale's Encyclopedia of Associations (Gale Research)
Hotel and Motel Red Book (American Hotel Association Directory Corp.)
Literary Market Place (Bowker)
Martindale-Hubbell Law Directory (Martindale-Hubbell)
Million Dollar Directory (Dun & Bradstreet)
N. Y. Ayer & Son's Directory of Newspapers and Periodicals (Ayer)
National Directory of Addresses and Telephone Numbers (Concord Reference Books)
Official Airline Guide (Official Airline Guides)
Official Congressional Directory (U.S. Government Printing Office)
Official Guide of the Railways (National Railway Publications Co.)
Patterson's American Education (Educational Directories)
The Standard Periodical Directory (Oxbridge)
Standard and Poor's Register of Corporations, Directors, and Executives of the United States and Canada (Standard and Poor's)
Thomas' Register of American Manufacturers (Thomas)
Ulrich's International Periodicals Directory (Bowker)
U.S. Government Manual (U.S. Government Printing Office)
Webster's Biographical Dictionary (Merriam)
Who's Who (various directories; Marquis)
Writer's Market (Writer's Digest)

ENCYCLOPEDIAS AND FACT BOOKS

Columbia Lippincott Gazetteer of the World (Columbia University Press)
Economic Almanac (Conference Board)
Encyclopaedia Britannica (Encyclopaedia Britannica)
Encyclopedia Americana (Americana Corp.)

Facts on File (Facts on File)

McGraw-Hill Encyclopedia of Science and Technology
  (McGraw-Hill)

New American Desk Encyclopedia (New American Library)

New Columbia Encyclopedia (Columbia University Press)

Statistical Abstract of the United States (U.S. Government
  Printing Office)

Statistical Yearbook (United Nations)

Van Nostrand's Scientific Encyclopedia (Van Nostrand)

The World Almanac and Book of Facts (Newspaper Enterprise Association)

INDEXES

Applied Science and Technology Index (Wilson)

Biography Index (Wilson)

Books in Print (Bowker)

Business Books and Serials in Print (Bowker)

Business Periodicals Index (Wilson)

Congressional Record Index (U.S. Government Printing
  Office)

Cumulative Book Index (Wilson)

Education Index (Wilson)

Guide to American Directories (Gale Research)

Guide to Reference Books (American Library Association)

Index to Legal Periodicals (Wilson)

Monthly Catalog of U.S. Government Publications (U.S.
  Government Printing Office)

New York Times Index (New York Times)

Paperback Books in Print (Bowker)

Public Affairs Information Service Bulletin (Public Affairs
  Information Service)

Reader's Guide to Periodical Literature (Wilson)

Social Science Index (Wilson)

Wall Street Journal Index (Dow Jones Books)

STYLE BOOKS

Associated Press Stylebook (Associated Press)
The Elements of Style (Macmillan)
Government Printing Office Style Manual (U.S. Government Printing Office)
The Gregg Reference Manual (McGraw-Hill)
The Chicago Manual of Style (University of Chicago Press)
Manual of Style and Usage (New York Times)
Mathematics into Type (American Mathematical Association)
The MLA Style Manual (Modern Language Association)
A Uniform System of Citation (Harvard Law Review Association)
Words into Type (Prentice-Hall)

NOTE: Always consult the latest edition of a work; most of the above works—and many more—are available in a well-stocked public, academic, or specialized library reference room. Write for information about procedures and rates in using any of the hundreds of databases available through the main utilities listed above; check current issues of computer magazines for reviews and sources of the rapidly expanding list of databases.

STANDARD SIZES OF COMMON PRINTED MATERIAL

BOOKS

5½ × 8½, 6⅛ × 9¼, 5 × 7⅜, 5⅜ × 8, 5½ × 8¼, 5⅝ × 8⅜

BROADSIDES

17 × 22, 19 × 25, 20 × 26, 23 × 35

FOLDERS

3½ × 6¼, 4 × 9, 5½ × 8½, 6 × 9, 8½ × 11, 9 × 12

FORMS

7 × 8½, 8½ × 11, 8½ × 14

CATALOG SHEETS

8½ × 11, 11 × 17

STATEMENTS

5½ × 8½, 7 × 8½

INVOICES

7 × 8½, 8½ × 11

LETTERHEADS

8½ × 11, 7¼ × 10½, 6 × 9, 5½ × 8½

BUSINESS CARDS

2 × 3½, 3½ × 4 (folder style)

ENVELOPES

Stationery: 4⅛ × 9½ (no. 10), 3⅞ × 8⅞ (no. 9), 3⅞ × 7½ (no. 8), 3⅝ × 6½ (no. 6¾), 3½ × 6 (no. 6¼), 4⅝ × 5⁵⁄₁₆ (no. 5)
Catalog and booklet: 6 × 9, 7 × 10, 8¾ × 11¼, 9 × 12, 9½ × 12½, 10 × 13

MAILING ADDRESS LABELS

3 × 5, 4 × 5

NOTE: Consult your printer for other sizes that may be available through local suppliers. See also **STANDARD PAPER WEIGHTS AND SIZES** in this chapter.

STANDARD PAPER WEIGHTS AND SIZES

Paper Classification	Standard Size (Inches)	Basis Weight (Pounds)
Book	25 × 38	30, 40, 45, 50, 60, 70, 80, 90, 100, 120
Bond	17 × 22	13, 16, 20, 24, 28, 32, 36, 40
Cover	20 × 26	50, 60, 65, 80, 90, 100
Bristol	22½ × 28½	57, 67, 80, 100, 120, 140, 160
Index	25½ × 30½	90, 110, 140, 170
Tag	24 × 36	100, 125, 150, 175, 200, 250

Source: International Paper Company, 891 New Brunswick Avenue, Rahway, NJ 07065.

NOTE: Basis weight refers to the weight of five hundred sheets (one ream) of paper in the standard size for that grade, or classification. See also **STANDARD SIZES OF COMMON PRINTED MATERIAL** in this chapter.

NUMBER OF WORDS AND EMS PER SQUARE INCH

Size of Type (Points)	Number of Words		Number of Ems
	Solid	Leaded	
5	69	50	207
6	47	34	144
8	32	23	81
10	21	16	52
11	17	14	43
12	14	11	36
14	11	8	26½

Source: United States Government Printing Office Style Manual (Washington, D.C.: U.S. Government Printing Office, March 1984).

NOTE: Em means the square of *any* body, or point, size of any letter. For example, a one-em dash (—) in ten-point type is ten points long.

PICAS AND EQUIVALENT INCHES

Picas	Inches		
1	0.166	or	3/16
2	.332		5/16
3	.498		8/16
4	.664		11/16
5	.830		13/16
6	.996		1
7	1.162		1 3/16
8	1.328		1 5/16
9	1.494		1 8/16
10	1.660		1 11/16
15	2.490		2 8/16
20	3.320		3 5/16
25	4.151		4 2/16
30	4.981		5
35	5.811		5 13/16
40	6.641		6 10/16
45	7.472		7 8/16
50	8.302		8 5/16
55	9.132		9 2/16
60	9.962		10
65	10.792		10 13/16
70	11.623		11 10/16
75	12.453		12 7/16
80	13.283		13 5/16
85	14.113		14 2/16
90	14.944		15
95	15.774		15 12/16
100	16.604		16 10/16

NOTE: A pica is equal to 12 points: 6 picas = 72 points = about 1 inch. To convert decimals (tenths) to standard ruler fractions (sixteenths), multiply the decimal component in column 2 above by 16. For example, to convert 1.660 inches to sixteenths of an inch, follow this procedure:

1. $0.660 \times 16 = 10.56$
2. Round 10.56 to 11.
3. $1.660 = 1^{11}/_{16}$

ARABIC AND ROMAN NUMERALS

I	1		XL	40
II	2		L	50
III	3		LX	60
IV	4		LXX	70
V	5		LXXX	80
VI	6		XC	90
VII	7		C	100
VIII	8		CC	200
IX	9		CCC	300
X	10		CD	400
XI	11		D	500
XII	12		DC	600
XIII	13		DCC	700
XIV	14		DCC	800
XV	15		CM	900
XVI	16		M	1,000
XVII	17		MM	2,000
XVIII	18		MMM	3,000
XIX	19		MV̄	4,000
XX	20		V̄	5,000
XXX	30			

NOTE: Repeating a letter repeats its value: XX = 20. A letter placed after one of greater value adds to it: LX = 60. A letter placed before one of greater value subtracts from it: XL = 40. A dash line over a numeral multiplies the value by 1,000: X̄ = 10,000.

METRIC CONVERSION TABLE

When You Know	Multiply by	To Find

Length

inches (in.)	2.54	centimeters (cm)
feet (ft.)	30.00	centimeters (cm)
yards (yd.)	0.90	meters (m)
miles (mi.)	1.60	kilometers (km)
millimeters (mm)	0.04	inches (in.)
centimeters (cm)	0.40	inches (in.)
meters (m)	3.30	feet (ft.)
meters (m)	1.10	yards (yd.)
kilometers (km)	0.60	miles (mi.)

Area

square inches (in.^{2})	6.50	square centimeters (cm^2)
square feet (ft.^{2})	0.09	square meters (m^2)
square yards (yd.^{2})	0.80	square meters (m^2)
square miles (mi.^{2})	2.60	square kilometers (km^2)
acres	0.40	hectares (ha)
square centimeters (cm^2)	0.16	square inches (in.^{2})
square meters (m^2)	1.20	square yards (yd.^{2})
square kilometers (km^2)	0.40	square miles (mi.^{2})
hectares (ha) (10,000 m^2)	2.50	acres

When You Know	*Multiply by*	*To Find*

Weight

ounces (oz.)	28.00	grams (g)
pounds (lb.)	0.45	kilograms (kg)
short tons (2,000 lbs.)	0.90	tonnes (t)
long tons (2,240 lbs.)	1.01	tonnes (t)
grams (g)	0.035	ounces (oz.)
kilograms (kg)	2.20	pounds (lb.)
tonnes (1,000 kg)	1.10	short tons
tonnes (1,000 kg)	0.98	long tons

Volume

teaspoons (tsp.)	5.00	milliliters (ml)
tablespoons (tbsp.)	15.00	milliliters (ml)
fluid ounces (fl. oz.)	30.00	milliliters (ml)
cups (c)	0.24	liters (l)
pints (pt.)	0.47	liters (l)
quarts (qt.)	0.95	liters (l)
gallons, U.S. (gal.)	3.80	liters (l)
gallons, Imp. (gal.)	4.50	liters (l)
cubic feet (ft.^{3})	0.028	cubic meters (m^3)
cubic yards (yd.^{3})	0.76	cubic meters (m^3)
milliliters (ml)	0.03	fluid ounces (fl. oz.)
liters (l)	2.10	pints (pt.)
liters (l)	1.06	quarts (qt.)
liters (l)	0.26	gallons, U.S. (gal.)
liters (l)	0.22	gallons, Imp. (gal.)
cubic meters (m^3)	35.00	cubic feet (ft.^{3})
cubic meters (m^3)	1.30	cubic yards (yd.^{3})

DIACRITICAL MARKS

´	Acute accent
`	Grave accent
˘	Breve
ˇ	Haček
¨	Diaresis
^ or ˆ or ¯	Circumflex
˜	Tilde
¯	Macron
¸	Cedilla

GREEK ALPHABET

Alphabet and pronunciation

Α	α	*𝒜a*	alpha	*a* in *father*
Β	β	*ℬℓ*	beta	*v*
Γ	γ	*𝒯γ*	gamma	*y* in *yes* before αι, ε, ει, η, ι, οι, ν, υι; *ng* in *singer* before γ, κ, ξ, χ; somewhat like *g* in *go* everywhere else
Δ	δ	*𝒟δ*	delta	*th* in *this*, except in νδρ, pronounced *ndr*
Ε	ε	*ℰε*	epsilon	*e* in *met*
Ζ	ζ	*𝒵ζ*	zeta	*z*
Η	η	*ℋη*	eta	*ee* in *eel*; *y* in *yet*; when after a consonant and before a vowel
Θ	θ	*𝒩ϑ*	theta	*th* in *thin*
Ι	ι	*𝒥ι*	iota	*ee* in *eel*; *y* in *yet* when initial or after a consonant, before a vowel
Κ	κ	*𝒦κ*	kappa	*k*
Λ	λ	*𝒜λ*	lambda	*l*
Μ	μ	*ℳμ*	mu	*m*
Ν	ν	*𝒩ν*	nu	*n*
Ξ	ξ	*𝒳ξ*	xi	*x* (= *ks*)

O	o	*O o*	omicron	o in *for*
Π	π	*π σ*	pi	p
P	ρ	*P ρ*	rho	r, somewhat like the Scotch trilled r
Σ	σς*	*Σ σ ς*	sigma	before β, γ, δ, λ, μ, ν, ρ; *s* everywhere else
T	τ	*T (τ)*	tau	
Υ	υ	*V υ*	upsilon	*e* in *eel*; *y* in *yet*, after a consonant and before a vowel
Φ	φ	*Φ φ*	phi	*j*
X	χ	*X α*	chi	like a strong *h* (like German *ch*)
Ψ	ψ	*Ψ ψ*	psi	*ps*
Ω	ω	*Ω ω*	omega	o in *or*

Source: United States Government Printing Office Style Manual (Washington, D.C.: U.S. Government Printing Office, March 1984).

* The character σ is used in initial and medial positions in a word. The character ς is used in the final position.

FAMILIAR FOREIGN WORDS

abaca
aide memoire
a la carte
a la king
a la mode
a priori
ad hoc
ad infinitum
alma mater
angstrom
aperitif
appliqué
apropos
auto(s)-da-fé
barranca
blasé
bona fide
boutonniere
brassiere
cabana
cafe
cafeteria
caïque
canapé
carte blanche
cause célèbre
château
cliche
cloisonné
comedienne
communiqué
confrere
consommé
cortege

coulee
coup de grace
coup d'état
coupe
creme
crepe
crepe de chine
debacle
debris
debut
debutante
décolleté
dejeuner
denouement
depot
dos-à-dos
éclair
éclat
ecru
effendi
élan
elite
entree
étude
ex officio
facade
faience
fazenda
fete
fiancé
frappe
garcon
glace
grille

gruyere
habeas corpus
habitué
ingenue
jardiniere
laissez faire
litterateur
materiel
matinee
mea culpa
mélange
melee
ménage
mésalliance
metier
moire
naive
naivete
nee
non sequitur
opéra bouffe
opéra comique
papier mâché
pasha
per annum
per se
pièce de résistance
Pleiade
porte cochere
porte lumière
portiere
pousse café
premiere
prima facie

pro rata	resume	status quo
pro tem	risqué	suede
protégé	rôle	table d'hôte
puree	rotisserie	tête-à-tête
quid pro quo	roué	tragedienne
rale	sauté	trattoria
recherché	séance	vice versa
regime	senor	vicuna
remuda	smorgasbord	vis-à-vis
rendezvous	soiree	weltschmerz
repertoire	soufflé	

NOTE: Although in contemporary writing familiar foreign words and anglicized words need not be italicized and do not require diacritical marks, follow the practices in your profession in these matters.

CONTEMPORARY ABBREVIATION$

General Abbreviations

A	answer
aa	author's alteration(s)
abbr.	abbreviated; abbreviation
abr.	abridged; abridgment
a/d	after date
a.d.	before the day
A.D.	in the year of our lord (*Anno Domini*)
ad fin.	to or at the end (*ad finem*)
ad inf.	without limit (*ad infinitum*)
ad init.	at the beginning (*ad initium*)
ad int.	in the meantime (*ad interim*)
ad lib.,	at one's pleasure; freely to the quantity
ad libit.	or amount desired (*ad libitum*)

ad loc.	to or at the place (*ad locum*)
ad val., a/v	according to value (*ad valorem*)
adj.	adjective
adv.	adverb
aka	also known as
a.m.	before noon (*ante meridiem*)
anon.	anonymous
a/o	account of
a to oc	attached to other correspondence
app.	appendix
art.	article
as.	at sight
a/s	after sight
AST	Atlantic standard time
att.	attached
attn., atten.	attention
au.	author
AV	authorized version
b	born; brother
bal.	balance
B.C.	before Christ
bf	boldface; brief (legal)
bibl.	library (*bibliotheca*)
bibliog.	bibliography
biog.	biography
bkt.	bracket
bo	branch office; back order
b/p	blueprint
Bros.	Brothers
bs	backspace
bw	please turn page (*bittle werden*)
©, copr.	copyright
c	carat; chapter(s); about (*circa*)

c. and s.c.	capital letters and small capitals (caps and small caps)
ca, c.	about (*circa*)
cal.	calendar; caliber
can.	canceled; cancellation
caps	capital letters
cert., ctf.	certified; certificate; certification
cf.	compare (*confer*)
ch.	chapter; chart
chap., chaps.	chapter(s)
chg.	change; charge
cir.	circular; circulation; circumference
cl	center line
CLT	code language telegram
co.	company; county
c/o	in care of; cash order
COD	cash, or collect, on delivery
col.	column
colloq.	colloquial
comp.	compiler; compiled by
con.	against (*contra*)
conj.	conjunction
cont.	continued
corp.	corporation; corporal; to the body (*corpori*)
CST	central standard time
CT	central time
ctn.	carton
ctr.	center; counter
cum.	with; cumulative
cur.	current
d	died; daughter
dba	doing business as (co. name)
dec.	decision; decimal
def.	definition
deg.	degree(s)

dept.	department
dia., diam.	diameter
diag.	diagram; diagonal
dict.	dictionary
div.	division
DL	day letter (telegraph)
dld	delivered
DLO	dead letter office
do.	ditto (the same)
d/s	days after sight
D.V.	God willing (*Deo volente*)
dy	delivery
ea.	each
eaon	except as otherwise noted
ed.	editor; edition(s); edited by; education
Ed. Note	editorial note
EDP	electronic data processing
EDT	eastern daylight time
EE	errors excepted; Early English
e.g.	for example (*exempli gratia*)
enc.	enclosure
ency.,	
encyc.	encyclopedia
end.	endorse; endorsement
eng.	engraved; engineer; engineering, engine
Eng.	English
eo	by authority of his office (*ex officio*)
eod	every other day (advertising)
e&oe	errors and omissions excepted
eohp	except as otherwise herein provided
esp.	especially
Esq.	esquire
est.	estimated; estate
EST	eastern standard time
eta	estimated time of arrival
et al.	and others (*et alii*)

etc.	and the others; and so forth (*et cetera*)
et seq.	and the following (*et sequens*)
ex	out of or from; without or not including
ex.	example
exp.	express; expenses
f.	following (after a numeral; *pl.* ff.); feminine
fac.	facsimile; fast as can
FD	free delivery; free dispatch
Fed. Reg.	*Federal Register*
ff	following (after a numeral); folios
fig(s).	figure(s)
fl.	flourished (*floruit*)
fn.	footnote
fo	firm offer
foc	free of charge
fol.	folio; following
fr.	from
Fr.	French
frt.	freight
fv.	on the back of the page (*folio verso*)
fwd	forward
fx	foreign exchange
FYI	for your information (interoffice use)
gen.	genus
ger.	gerund
GI	government issue; general issue
Gk.	Greek
GNP	gross national product
gro.	gross
hdqs.,	
hq., HQ	headquarters
hdwe.	hardware
hon.	honorable
hr.	hour(s)

HR	House bill (federal); House of Representatives
hyp.	hypothesis
ibid.	in the same place (*ibidem*)
id.	the same (*idem*)
i.e.	that is (*id est*)
in pr.	in the beginning (*in principio*)
in re	in regard to
Inc.	Incorporated
incl.	inclusive
inf.	infinity; below (*infra*)
int.	interest
introd.	introduction
IQ	intelligence quotient
ital.	italics
l. (*pl.* ll)	line (s)
L	Latin
L. Ed.	Lawyers Edition
L/A	letter of authority
lat.	latitude
lc	lowercase
LC	deferreds (cable messages)
lf	lightface; ledger folio
lmsc	let me see correspondence
loc. cit.	in the place cited (*loco citato*)
log.	logarithm
long.	longitude
loq.	he/she speaks (*loquitur*)
ls	place of the seal (*locus sigilli*)
LT	letter message (cables)
Ltd.	limited (British)
lv.	leave
m	married; masculine
M	thousand; monsieur (*pl.* MM); noon (*meridies*)
max.	maximum

MC	master of ceremonies; member of Congress
med.	medium; medicine; medical
Messrs.	Misters (Messieurs)
mfg.	manufacturing
min.	minimum; minute(s)
misc.	miscellaneous
Mlle.	Mademoiselle
mm	necessary changes being made (*mutatis mutandis*)
MM	Messieurs
Mme.	Madame
Mmes.	Mesdames
mo	money order
mo.	month(s)
MP	member of Parliament; military police
ms(s)., MS(S)	manuscript(s)
Msgr.	Monsignor: Monseigneur
mst.	measurement
MST	mountain standard time
n	note (*pl.* nn); number; net; born
NA, N/A	not available
natl., nat'l	national
n.b., N.B.	note well (*nota bene*)
NCO	noncommissioned officer
nd, n.d.	no date
ne	not exceeding
nes	not elsewhere specified
NG	no good
NL	night letter (telegraph)
NLT	night letter cable
NM	night message
N/m	no mark
no.	number
noe	not otherwise enumerated
nohp	not otherwise herein provided
nom.	nominative; nominal

nom. std.	nominal standard
non obs.	notwithstanding (*non obstante*)
non pros.	does not prosecute (*non prosequitur*)
non seq.	does not follow (*non sequitur*)
nop	not otherwise provided for
nos	not otherwise specified
np, n.p.	no place; no publisher
NP	notary public
ns	new series
NS, N.S.	New Style(dates)
nspf	not specially provided for
ntp	no title page
ob.	died (*obiit*)
obs.	obsolete
oc	office copy
oe	omissions excepted
OE	Old English
oo	on order
o/o	order of
op	out of print
op. cit.	in the work cited (*opere citato*)
opn.	opinion
os, o.s.	old series
o/s	out of stock
OS, O.S.	one side; Old Style
p.	page (*pl.* pp.)
pa	by the year (*per annum*); power of attorney
pam.	pamphlet
par.	paragraph
pass.	throughout (*passim*)
pat.	patent
pc, pct., %	percent
pd	per diem
pd.	passed; paid

pkg.	package
pl.	plural; plate
p&l	profit and loss
p.m.	afternoon (*post meridiem*)
PM	postmaster
p/n	please note
PO	post office
pp	parcel post
pp.	pages
ppd.	prepaid; postpaid
ppi	parcel post insured
pr.	pair
pref.	preface; preferred
prep.	preposition
princ.	principle; principal
pro tem.	for the time being (*pro tempore*)
prox.	proximate; of the next month (*proximo*)
P.S.	postscript
PST	Pacific standard time
PT	Pacific time
pub.	publication; publisher; published by
	question; query
Q.E.D.,	which was to be proved or demonstrated
q.e.d.	(*quod erat demonstrandum*)
qq	questions; queries
qr.	quarter
q.v.	which see (*quod vide*)
r	recto; reigned
R/A	return to author
R/C	recovered; reconsigned
rcd.	received
re	in regard to
recd., rec'd	received
ref.	reference; referred; referee
reg.	registered; regulation(s)

rep.	report
repr.	reprint; reprinted
res.	research; residue; reserve; residence; resigned; resolution
rev.	review; revised; revision
rm.	ream (paper); room(s)
rom.	roman (type)
rop	run of paper
rotn. no.	rotation number
rp	reply paid (cable)
RSVP	please reply (*répondez, s'il vous plaît*)
s	substantive; son
/s/	signed
sa	without year (*sine anno*); under the year (*sub anno*); subject to approval
sc	small capital letters (small caps); namely, to wit (*scilicet*); scene
sd	without a day being named (*sine die*)
sec(s).	section(s)
seq.	the following; in sequence
ser.	series
sg., sing.	singular
sgd.	signed
shpt.	shipment
sic	so; thus (to confirm a word that might be questioned)
sl	without place (*sine loco*)
soc.	society
sol.	solution
SOP	standard operating procedure
sp	supra protest
ss	namely (*scilicet*)
st.	stanza; street
St.	saint
sta.	station
stat.	statute(s)

std.	standard
stg.	sterling; storage
sup.	above (*supra*)
supp.,	
suppl.	supplement
s.v.	same year; under the word (*sub verbo; pl.* s.vv.)
svp	if you please (*s'il vous plaît*)
syn.	synonymous
taw	twice a week (advertising)
tb	time base
tel.	telegram; telegraph; telephone
tf	till forbidden (advertising)
tm	trademark; true mean
tr.	transpose
trans.	transitive; translated; transportation; transaction
ts	typescript
twp.	township
U, univ.	university
uc	uppercase
ud	as directed
ugt.	urgent (cable)
ui	as below (*ut infra*)
ult.	of the last month (*ultimo*)
up.	under proof
u.s., ut	
sup.	as above (*ut supra*)
usw.	and so forth (*und so weiter*)
ut	universal time
v	value
v.	verse (*pl.* vv.); verb; versus; verso
v.i.	see below (*vide infra*)
vid.	see (*vide*)
viz.	namely (*videlicet*)

vol.	volume
vs., v.	versus
vv	vice versa
wa	will advise
wd.	word; warranted
wf	wrong font (typesetting)
wk.	week
wp, WP	word processing; without prejudice
wpp	waterproof paper packing
xp	express paid
yb.	yearbook
yr.	year
z.	zone; zero

NOTE: Authorities differ in matters of capitalization and punctuation of abbreviations. When appropriate, follow the practices in your profession or the preferred style in your office. General abbreviations (and symbols) such as *p.* for *page* and % for *percent* should not be used in written text discussion but are commonly used in supplementary elements such as footnotes and tables. Abbreviations of words such as *ugt.* for *urgent* should not be used at all in finished copy, but some writers use such short forms in note taking as a type of shorthand. See **ABBREVIATION GUIDELINES** in Chapter 1 for tips on matters such as proper use of capitalization and punctuation.

Technical Abbreviations

a, amp.	ampere
Å	angstrom
ac	alternating current
af	audiofrequency

a-h	ampere-hour
a/m	ampere per meter
AM	amplitude modulation
at.	atmosphere
at. no.	atomic number
at. vol.	atomic volume
at. wt.	atomic weight
au	astronomical unit
Au	gold
av., avdp.	avoirdupois
a/w	actual weight
bbl	barrel
bbl/d, b/d	barrel per day
bdl	bundle
bhp	brake horsepower
bl	bale(s)
bm	board measure
bp	boiling point
Btu, BTU	British thermal unit
bu.	bushel
c	cycle (radio)
C	Celsius; Centigrade; centi (prefix: one-hundredth)
C/	case(s)
cal.	small calories
cd.	cord
cd. ft.	cord foot
cg	centigram
ch, c-h	candle-hour(s)
cl	centiliter
cm	centimeter
c/m	cycles per minute
cm^2	square centimeter
cm^3	cubic centimeter
cp	candlepower

d	deci (prefix: one-tenth)
da	deka (prefix: ten)
dag	dekagram
dal	dekaliter
dam	dekameter
dam^2	square dekameter
dam^3	cubic dekameter
dB	decibel
dBu	decibel unit
dc	direct current
dg	decigram
dl	deciliter
dm	decimeter
dm^2	square decimeter
dm^3	cubic decimeter
dr.	dram
dw	dead weight
dwc	dead weight capacity
dwt	deadweight ton(s); pennyweight(s)
dyn	dyne
EHF	extremely high frequency
EMF	electromotive force
esu	electrostatic unit
eV	electron volt
F	Fahrenheit; farad
fbm	board foot; board foot measure
FM	frequency modulation
ft.	foot
ft.^{2}	square foot
ft.^{3}	cubic foot
ft. H_2O	conventional foot of water
g	gram; gravity
G	gauss; giga (prefix: one million)

gal.	gallon
GeV	gigaelectronvolt
GHz	gigahertz
h	hecto (prefix: one hundred)
H	henry
ha	hectare
hf	high frequency
hg	hectogram
hl	hectoliter
hm	hectometer
hm^2	square hectometer
hm^3	cubic hectometer
hp	horsepower
Hz	hertz
ihp	indicated horsepower
in.	inch
in.^{2}	square inch
in.^{3}	cubic inch
J	joule
k	kilo (prefix: one thousand); knot; carat
kc	kilocycle
keV	kiloelectronvolt
kg	kilogram
kG	kilogauss
kgf	kilogram-force
kHz	kilohertz
kl	kiloliter
km	kilometer
km^2	square kilometer
km^3	cubic kilometer
kn	knot (speed)
kt	kiloton; carat
kV	kilovolt

kVa	kilovoltampere
kW	kilowatt
kWh	kilowatt-hour
l	liter
lf	low frequency
lin. ft.	linear foot
l/m	lines per minute
l/s	lines per second
m	meter; milli (prefix: one-thousandth)
m^2	square meter
m^3	cubic meter
M	mega (prefix: one million); thousand
ma	milliampere
mbar	millibar
mc	millicycle
Mc	megacycle
MeV	megaelectronvolts
mF	millifarad
mg	milligram
mG	milligauss
mH	millihenry
mHz	millihertz
MHz	megahertz
mi.	mile (statute)
mi.^{2}	square mile
mi./hr., mi/h	mile(s) per hour
min.	minute (time)
ml	milliliter
mm	millimeter
mm^2	square millimeter
mm^3	cubic millimeter
ms	millisecond
Mt	megaton
mV	millivolt
mW	milliwatt

MW	megawatt
μ	micro (prefix: one-millionth)
μF	microfarad
μg	microgram
μH	microhenry
μin.	microinch
μm	micrometer
μs	microsecond
μV	microvolt
μW	microwatt
n	nano (prefix: one-billionth)
na	nanoampere
nhp	nominal horsepower
nm	nanometer
nmi.	nautical mile
npt	nominal pressure and temperature
ns	nanosecond
oz.	ounce (avoirdupois)
p	pico (prefix: one-trillionth)
pc, pct., %	percent
pk.	peck
p/m	parts per million
ps	picosecond
pt.	pint
pW	picowatt
ql	quintal
qt.	quart
R	rankine; roentgen
rf	radio frequency
r/min.	revolutions per minute
rms	root mean square
r/s	revolutions per second

s	second (time)
sh. tn.	short ton
shp	shaft horsepower
sw	shipper's weights
T	tera (prefix: one trillion); tesla
tMW	thermal megawatt
u	atomic mass unit
uhf	ultrahigh frequency
V	volt
Va	volt ampere
vhf	very high frequency
V/m	volt per meter
W	watt
Wh	watt-hour
yd.	yard
yd.^{2}	square yard
yd.^{3}	cubic yard
z	zero hour

NOTE: Although technical abbreviations are widely used in technical material, they should be used sparingly, if at all, in nontechnical writing (for example, say "twenty-five kilometers," not "25 km"); see **ABBREVIATION GUIDELINES** in Chapter 1. See also **Computer Abbreviations and Acronyms** for additional examples of technical abbreviations.

Computer Abbreviations and Acronyms

ABM	automated batch mixing
abort	abandon activity
ABP	actual block processor
abs	absolute
AC	automatic/analog computer
ACC	accumulator
ACF	advanced communication function
ACL	Audit Command Language
ACM	area composition machine
ADAPS	automatic displayed plotting system
ADC	analog-to-digital converter
ADIS	automatic data interchange system
ADP	automatic/advanced data processing
ADR	address; adder; analog-to-digital recorder
ADV	advance
AFR	automatic field/format recognition
ALCOM	algebraic computer/compiler
ALGOL	Algorithmic Language
ALP	automated language processing
ALU	arithmetic and logic unit
ANACOM	analog computer
AOC	automatic output control
AP	attached processor
APL	A Programming Language
APT	Automatic Programmed Tools (language)
AQL	acceptable quality level
ARQ	automatic repeat request; automatic request for correction
ARU	audio response unit
ASC	automatic sequence control
ASCII	American Standard Code for Information Interchange
ASDI	automated selective dissemination of information
ASM	auxiliary storage management

ASP	attached support processor
ASR	answer, send, and receive
ATLAS	Automatic Tabulating, Listing, and Sorting System
AUTODIN	automated digital network
B	bit; magnetic flux density
BA	binary add
BAM	basic access method
BASIC	Beginner's All-Purpose Symbolic Instruction
BC	binary code
BCD	binary-coded decimal
BDU	basic device/display unit
BIM	beginning of information marker
bit	binary digit
BIU	basic information unit
BN	binary number system
BOF	beginning of file
BOS	basic operating system
BOT	beginning of tape
bpi	bits per inch
bps	bits per second
BPS	basic programming support
BS	backspace character
BTU	basic transmission unit
C	computer; compute; control
CA	channel adapter
CAD	computer-aided design
CAD/CAM	computer-aided design/computer-aided manufacturing
CAI	computer-aided instruction
CAI/OP	computer analog input/output
CAL	computer-aided learning
CAM	computer-aided manufacturing
CAN	cancel character
CAR	computer-assisted retrieval

CAT	computer-assisted training/teaching
CDC	call directing code
CHAR	character
CIM	computer-input microfilm
CIOCS	communications input/output control system
CIU	computer interface unit
CLAT	communication line adapter
CLK	clock
CLT	communication line terminal
CMC	code for magnetic characters
CMND	command; instruction
CMS	conversation monitor system
CNC	computer numerical control
COBOL	Common Business-Oriented Language
COL	Computer-Oriented Language
COM	computer-output microfilm
CP	central processor
cph	characters per hour
cpm	characters per minute; cards per minute; critical path method
CP/M	controlled program monitor; control program/ microcomputers
CPS	conversational programming system; central processing system
CPU	central processing unit
cr	carriage return
CR	call request; control relay
CRAM	card random access method
CROM	control read-only memory
CRT	cathode ray tube
CSL	Computer-Sensitive Language
CST	channel status table
CTR	computer tape reader
CTU	central terminal unit
CU	control unit
CWP	communicating word processor

DAA	direct-access arrangement
DAC	data acquisition and control; digital/analog converter
DASD	direct-access storage device
DBAM	database access method
DBMS	database management system
DD	digital data
DDL	Data-Description Language
DDS	digital-display scope
DE	display element
DIP	dual in-line package
DLC	data-link control
DMA	direct memory access
DNC	direct numerical control
DOS	disk operating system
DOV	data over voice
DP	data processing
DRL	Data-Retrieval Language
DRO	destructive readout
DTR	data terminal ready
DUV	data under voice
EDP	electronic data processing
EOF	end of file
EOJ	end of job
EOP	end of paragraph
EOR	end of record/run
ESI	externally specified index
ETB	end of transmission block
F	feedback
FACT	Fully Automatic Compiling Technique
FDOS	floppy-disk operating system
FF	flip-flop
FIRST	fast interactive retrieval system
FORTRAN	Formula Translation (language)

GDT	graphic display terminal
GP	general program
GPC	general-purpose computer
GPR	general-purpose register
HSM	high-speed memory
HSP	high-speed printer
HSR	high-speed reader
IC	integrated circuit; input circuit
ID	identification
I/O	input/output
IOB	input-output buffer
IOC	input-output controller
ipm	impulses per minute
IR	infrared
ISR	information storage and retrieval
k	about a thousand (in storage capacity)
KB	keyboard
kb	kilobytes
KSR	keyboard send and receive
LCD	liquid crystal display
LIFO	last in, first out
LILO	last in, last out
LP	linear programming
lpm	lines per minute
lsc	least significant character
lsd	least significant digit
M	mega
mag	magnetic
Mb	megabyte
MC	master control
MCP	master control program
MIS	management information system

MPS	microprocessor system
msc	most significant character
msd	most significant digit
MSU	modem-sharing unit
MT	machine translation
MUX	multiplexer
n	nano-
NAM	network access machine
NAU	network addressable unit
NC	numerical control
NCP	network control program
NL	new-line character
NO-OP	no-operation instruction
ns	nanosecond
OCR	optical character recognition
ODB	output to display buffer
OEM	original equipment manufacturer
OLRT	on-line real time
OP	operations
opm	operations per minute
OR	operations research
OS	operating system
OSI	open-system interconnection
P	pico-
PA	paper advance
PC	program counter
PCI	process control interface
PCM	punch-card machine
PCS	punched-card system
PDN	public data network
PERT	program evaluation and review technique
PIO chip	programmable input/output chip
PIU	path information unit
PRT	production-run tape

RAM	random-access memory
RAX	remote access
READ	real-time electronic access and display
REM	recognition memory
ROM	read-only memory
RT	real time
RTU	remote terminal unit
R/W	read/write
RWM	read-write memory
RZ	return to zero
SAM	sequential-access method; serial-access memory
S/F	store and forward
SLT	solid-logic technology
SOP	standard operating procedure
STX	start of text
TLU	table lookup
TOS	tape operating system
UCS	user control storage
USASCII	USA Standard Code for Information Interchange
VDI	video display input
VDT	video display terminal
WC	write and compute
WFL	work-flow language
WIP	work in progress
WO	write out
wp, WP	word processor
WS	working storage/space
XMT	transmit

NOTE: See also **Technical Abbreviations.**

Organizations

AA	Alcoholics Anonymous
AAA	American Automobile Association
ABA	American Booksellers Association; American Bankers Association; American Bar Association
ABC	American Broadcasting Company
AEC	Atomic Energy Commission
ALA	Author's League of America
AFL-CIO	American Federation of Labor–Congress of Industrial Organizations
AG	Author's Guild
AIB	American Institute of Banking
AID	Agency for International Development
AMA	American Medical Association
AP	Associated Press
ARC	American (National) Red Cross
ARS	Agricultural Research Service
ASA	American Standards Association; American Statistical Association
ASTA	American Society of Travel Agents
BLS	Bureau of Labor Statistics
BTA	Board of Tax Appeals
CAP	Civil Air Patrol
CBS	Columbia Broadcasting System
CCC	Commodity Credit Corporation
CEA	Commodity Exchange Administration
CEC	Commodity Exchange Commission
CED	Committee for Economic Development
CIA	Central Intelligence Agency
CID	Criminal Investigation Department
CORE	Congress of Racial Equality
CPSC	Consumer Product Safety Commission
CSC	Civil Service Commission

EEC	European Economic Community
EEOC	Equal Employment Opportunity Commission
EPA	Environmental Protection Agency
FAA	Federal Aviation Agency
FBI	Federal Bureau of Investigation
FCA	Farm Credit Administration
FCC	Federal Communications Commission
FDA	Food and Drug Administration
FDIC	Federal Deposit Insurance Corporation
FHA	Federal Housing Administration
FMC	Federal Maritime Commission
FPC	Federal Power Commission
FRB	Federal Reserve Board; Federal Reserve Bank
FRS	Federal Reserve System
FSA	Federal Security Agency
FTC	Federal Trade Commission
GAO	General Accounting Office
GHQ	General Headquarters (Army)
GPO	Government Printing Office
GSA	General Services Administration
HHFA	Housing and Home Finance Agency
HUD	Housing and Urban Development (Department of)
ICC	Interstate Commerce Commission
IFC	International Finance Corporation
IFTU	International Federation of Trade Unions
ILO	International Labor Organization
ILP	Independent Labour Party (British)
IMF	International Monetary Fund
INP	International News Photos
INS	International News Service
IRO	International Refugee Organization
IRS	Internal Revenue Service

ITO	International Trade Organization
IWW	Industrial Workers of the World
KC	Knights of Columbus
KKK	Ku Klux Klan
LC	Library of Congress
NAACP	National Assocation for the Advancement of Colored People
NALS	National Association of Legal Secretaries
NAM	National Association of Manufacturers
NAS	National Academy of Sciences
NASA	National Aeronautics and Space Administration
NATO	North Atlantic Treaty Organization
NBC	National Broadcasting Company
NBS	National Broadcasting Service
NEA	National Education Association; National Editorial Association
NIH	National Institutes of Health
NLRB	National Labor Relations Board
NMB	National Mediation Board
NOW	National Organization for Women
NPS	National Park Service
NRC	Nuclear Regulatory Commission
NSC	National Security Council
NSF	National Science Foundation
OAS	Organization of American States
OECD	Organization for Economic Cooperation and Development
OMB	Office of Management and Budget
PBS	Public Broadcasting Service
PHA	Public Housing Administration

PHS	Public Health Service
PSI	Professional Secretaries International
REA	Rural Electrification Administration
ROTC	Reserve Officers' Training Corp
RRB	Railroad Retirement Board
SBA	Small Business Administration
SEATO	Southeast Asia Treaty Organization
SEC	Securities and Exchange Commission
SSA	Social Security Administration
SSS	Selective Service System
TC	Tax Court of the United States
TVA	Tennessee Valley Authority
UN	United Nations
UNESCO	United Nations Educational, Scientific, and Cultural Organization
USIA	United States Information Agency
UNICEF	United Nations Children's Fund
UNRRA	United Nations Relief and Rehabilitation Administration
UPI	United Press International
UPS	United Parcel Service
USDA	United States Department of Agriculture
USIA	United States Information Agency
VA	Veterans Administration
VFW	Veterans of Foreign Wars
VISTA	Volunteers in Service to America
WHO	World Health Organization

NOTE: In informal writing, spell out most abbreviations of organizations the first time mentioned in the text and place the initials immediately after the name in parentheses, for example, Volunteers in Service to America (VISTA). There-after, you may use the initials alone. A few well-known organizations such as NATO and NAACP may be referred to by their initials alone without spelling out the name the first time mentioned.

Foreign Countries and Regions

Africa	Afr.
Albania	Alb.
Argentina	Argen.
Australia	Austl.
Austria	Aus.
Belgium	Belg.
Bolivia	Bol.
Brazil	Braz.
Burma	Burma
Canada	Can.
Chile	Chile
China	China
Colombia	Colom.
Czechoslovakia	Czech.
Denmark	Den.
Dominician Republic	Dom. Rep.
East Germany	E.Ger.
Ecuador	Ecuador
Egypt	Egypt
El Salvador	El. Sal.
Europe	Eur.
England	Eng.
Finland	Fin.
France	Fr.
Ghana	Ghana
Great Britain	Gr. Brit.
Greece	Greece
Guatemala	Guat.

Haiti	Haiti
Honduras	Hond.
Hong Kong	H.K.
Hungary	Hung.
Iceland	Ice.
India	India
Ireland	Ir.
Israel	Isr.
Italy	Italy
Japan	Japan
Korea	Korea
Luxembourg	Lux.
Mexico	Mex.
Netherlands	Neth.
New Zealand	N.Z.
Nicaragua	Nicar.
Nigeria	Nig.
Norway	Nor.
Pakistan	Pak.
Panama	Pan.
Paraguay	Para.
Philippines	Phil.
Poland	Pol.
Portugal	Port.
Rhodesia	Rhodesia
Romania	Rom.
Scotland	Scot.
South Africa	S.Afr.
Spain	Spain
Sweden	Swed.
Switzerland	Switz.
Turkey	Turk.
Uganda	Uganda
U.S.S.R.	U.S.S.R.
United Kingdom	U.K.
Uruguay	Uru.
Venezuela	Venez.

Wales	Wales
West Germany	W.Ger.
Yugoslavia	Yugo.
Zambia	Zambia
Zimbabwe	Zimb.

NOTE: Country names should be spelled out in general text discussion (except for the U.S.S.R., or USSR, which is more often abbreviated); however, the name should be abbreviated in footnotes and references, for example, Wyndham, Austl.

States

	Traditional	Postal
Alabama	Ala.	AL
Alaska	Alaska	AK
American Samoa*	Amer. Samoa	AS
Arizona	Ariz.	AZ
Arkansas	Ark.	AR
California	Calif.	CA
Canal Zone*	C.Z.	CZ
Colorado	Colo.	CO
Connecticut	Conn.	CT
Delaware	Del.	DE
District of Columbia	D.C.	DC
Florida	Fla.	FL
Georgia	Ga.	GA
Guam*	Guam	GU
Hawaii	Hawaii	HI
Idaho	Idaho	ID

	Traditional	*Postal*
Illinois	Ill.	IL
Indiana	Ind.	IN
Iowa	Iowa	IA
Kansas	Kans.	KS
Kentucky	Ky.	KY
Louisiana	La.	LA
Maine	Maine	ME
Maryland	Md.	MD
Massachusetts	Mass.	MA
Michigan	Mich.	MI
Minnesota	Minn.	MN
Mississippi	Miss.	MS
Missouri	Mo.	MO
Montana	Mont.	MT
Nebraska	Nebr.	NE
Nevada	Nev.	NV
New Hampshire	N.H.	NH
New Jersey	N.J.	NJ
New Mexico	N.Mex.	NM
New York	N.Y.	NY
North Carolina	N.C.	NC
North Dakota	N.Dak.	ND
Ohio	Ohio	OH
Oklahoma	Okla.	OK
Oregon	Oreg.	OR
Pennsylvania	Pa.	PA
Puerto Rico*	P.R.	PR
Rhode Island	R.I.	RI
South Carolina	S.C.	SC
South Dakota	S.Dak.	SD
Tennessee	Tenn.	TN
Texas	Tex.	TX
Utah	Utah	UT
Vermont	Vt.	VT
Virginia	Va.	VA

	Traditional	*Postal*
Virgin Islands*	V.I.	VI
Washington	Wash.	WA
West Virginia	W.Va.	WV
Wisconsin	Wis.	WI
Wyoming	Wyo.	WY

NOTE: Spell out names in general text discussion (Wyoming), but use the traditional abbreviation in footnotes and references (Riverton, Wyo.), and use the two-letter postal abbreviation in letter and envelope mailing addresses.

*U.S. territories and possessions (by treaty, the Panama Canal will revert to Panama by 1999). Guam and Puerto Rico are self-governing U.S. territories. American Samoa and three of the Virgin Islands (St. Croix, St. Thomas, St. John) are non-self-governing U.S. territories.

POSTAL REGULATIONS

Domestic Mail

EXPRESS MAIL®

Express service provides the fastest postal delivery for high-priority shipments within the United States and to certain foreign countries. For Express Mail Next Day Service, take shipments to any designated Express Mail Post Office by 5:00 p.m. Shipments are insured against loss or damage at no additional cost. Other services include Express Mail Same Day Airport Service, Custom Designed Service, and International Service.

FIRST-CLASS MAIL

Any mailable matter under twelve ounces may be sent as first-class mail. Postcards, personal correspondence, matter wholly or partially in writing or typewriting, bills, and statements of account *must* be mailed first class. First-class mail is delivered overnight locally and to certain designated areas if properly addressed (including zip code) and deposited by the specified collection time. To other locations, third-day delivery is provided. For an additional fee first-class mail may be registered or certified.

FIRST-CLASS PRESORT MAIL

The presort rate, which is less than the regular rate for letters and postcards, is charged on each piece that is part of a group of ten or more pieces sorted to the same five-digit zip code or a group of fifty or more pieces sorted to the same first three-digit zip code. Presort mail must consist of at least five hundred pieces. Mail that cannot be separated to five or three digits is counted toward the minimum volume but does not qualify for the lower rate. Customers must pay an annual fee to use the presort class of mail.

FIRST-CLASS ZONE-RATED (PRIORITY) MAIL

Rates for first-class mail over twelve ounces are based on six zoned distances. Generally, the maximum weight limit is seventy pounds; the maximum size is 108 inches, length and girth combined. Other weight and size limitations apply in cases of APO and FPO mail to and from the forty-eight contiguous states. For an additional fee, priority mail may be registered, certified, or insured.

SECOND-CLASS MAIL (NEWSPAPERS AND OTHER PERIODICALS)

Newspapers and other periodicals issued at least four times

a year may be sent as second-class mail. A second-class permit is required, and publishers must distribute primarily to paid subscribers; also, second-class publications may not be designed primarily for advertising purposes. The regular second-class postage rate varies depending on the distance mailed, the advertising portion of the publication's content, and whether the publication is mailed to an address within the county of publication. Anyone can mail individual complete copies of a second-class publication at the "transient" rate.

REQUESTER PUBLICATIONS MAIL

Publishers using the requester category may mail at second-class rates, whether the publication is free or paid for by subscribers. Each issue must contain at least twenty-four pages, and the publication must be issued at least four times a year; no issue may contain more than 75 percent advertising; the publication may not be used to promote the owners, controllers, or the mail business; also, there must be a list of persons who request the publication, with at least 50 percent of the copies going to them.

THIRD-CLASS MAIL (ADVERTISING MAIL AND MERCHANDISE WEIGHING LESS THAN ONE POUND)

Circulars, booklets, catalogs, and other printed materials not required to be sent at first-class mail and merchandise, farm products, and keys may be sent as third-class mail. Each piece must be less than sixteen ounces. Third-class mail is subject to postal inspection but may be sealed if clearly marked "Third Class" on the outside. Bulk-rate third-class mail requires a bulk-mail permit, for which an annual fee is charged, and applies to mailings of pieces separately addressed to different addresses in quantities of not less than two hundred pieces or fifty pounds. Pieces must be zipcoded, presorted, and bundled or sacked. For an additional fee, third-class mail may be insured and receive "special handling."

FOURTH-CLASS MAIL (PARCELS)

Parcels weighing one pound or more may be sent as fourth-class mail. Generally, parcels weighing a maximum of seventy pounds and measuring up to 108 inches in girth and length combined may be mailed anywhere in the United States. Other weight and size limitations apply in the case of APO and FPO mail to and from the forty-eight contiguous states. Packages should not be sealed unless you state on them that they may be opened for postal inspection. Special rates apply to books (various printed matter and manuscripts) and library materials (books, printed matter, recordings, and so on); packages must be clearly marked, for example, "Special Fourth-Class Rate—Manuscript." For an additional fee, fourth-class mail may be insured and receive "special handling."

International Mail

POSTAL UNION MAIL

LC mail (letters and cards) consists of letters, letter packages, aerogrammes, postcards, and postal cards. *AO mail* (other articles) includes printed matter, matter for the blind, and small packets.

LETTERS AND LETTER PACKAGES

Written or recorded communcations resembling actual and personal correspondence must be sent as letter mail. Unless prohibited by the country of destination, dutiable merchandise may be transmitted in packages prepaid at the letter rate. Typewritten material must be sent as "letters," not printed matter. Merchandise liable to customs duty may be forwarded in letters or letter packages to many countries, prepaid at the letter rate when permitted. Consult the post office regarding forms to be filled out, labels to be affixed, and various restrictions and requirements per country.

AEROGRAMMES

Sheets on which a message can be written and that can be folded in the form of an envelope and sealed are known as *aerogrammes*. They can be sent to all foreign countries at a uniform rate. No enclosures are allowed. Aerogrammes with printed postage and airmail markings are sold at all post offices. Those manufactured by private concerns, if approved by the U.S. Postal Service, may also be used.

POSTCARDS

Only single cards, not reply-paid cards or folded (double) cards, are allowed. The maximum size is 6 by 4¼ inches, and the minimum size is 5½ by 3½ inches. Rates vary by country, with surface or air rates applying. Ask your local post office for further details.

PRINTED MATTER

Printed matter in international mail is paper on which letters, words, characters, figures, or images, or any combination thereof, not having the character of actual or personal correspondence, have been reproduced in several identical copies by any process other than handwriting or typewriting.

Manuscripts of literary works or of newspapers and scores or sheets of music in manuscript are also admitted as "Printed Matter." *Regular printed matter* is all printed matter other than books, sheet music, and publisher's second-class and controlled-circulation publications. Printed matter may be sealed if postage is paid by permit imprint, postage-meter stamps, precanceled stamps, or second-class or controlled-circulation indicia. Material must be clearly marked (for example, "Printed Matter—Books"). Ask your local post office about further requirements.

MATTER FOR THE BLIND

Certain material up to fifteen pounds that is unsealed may be sent as matter for the blind. Air service is available to Canada for matter for the blind prepared as letters or letter packages and paid at the letter rate. To countries other than Canada, the AO rate applies. Ask your local post office for details concerning items admissible in international mail as matter for the blind.

SMALL PACKETS

The small-packet class is designed to permit the mailing of small items of merchandise and samples to countries that will accept them. Philatelic items may be mailed under this classification only to Canada. Postage rates are less than for letter packages or parcel post. The weight limit is two pounds in most countries. Write "Small Packet" on the wrapper. All packets must bear the green customs label Form 2976. Ask your local post office about restrictions, requirements, and available services per country.

PARCEL POST

Parcel post may be sent to almost every country in the world by either direct or indirect service. Parcels are sent from the United States by surface vessel or by airplane directly to the country of destination or first to an intermediate country, where they are subject to transit charges. Pack items in canvas or similar material, double-faced corrugated cardboard boxes, solid fiber boxes or cases, thick cardboard boxes, or strong wooden boxes of material at least half an inch thick. Ask your local post office about restrictions, requirements, and available services per country.

NOTE: Both domestic and international regulations are subject to change, and numerous restrictions apply, especially in the case of international mail.

GLOSSARY

aa. Author's alteration; a change that an author makes after manuscript has been typset.

Acetate overlay. A transparent sheet of clear plastic, placed over original *artwork* or *copy*, that shows separations of color and of *line drawings* and *halftones*.

Agate line. A standard unit of measure often used by newspapers and magazines in measuring advertising space (fourteen agate lines = one *column inch*).

Airbrush. An instrument that functions like a small spray gun, used to create an artistic effect and to retouch photographs.

Artwork. Illustrations (for example, drawings) prepared for reproduction.

Artype. Various *typefaces* printed on transparent sheets that can be removed and used on *artwork*. See *Burnishing*.

Ascender. The stem of a *lowercase* (small) letter, such as *b, d, f, h, k, l,* and *t,* that extends above the main body of the letter.

Back matter. Material following the text (for example, appendix, index); also called end matter.

Backbone. The bound edge of a book; also called the spine.

Backing up. *Printing* on the reverse side of a sheet that is already printed on one side.

Base line. The horizontal alignment of the base of capital letters.

Basis weight. The designation of paper in pounds based on the weight of a *ream*, or five hundred sheets, of paper in the standard size for the particular grade of paper.

Benday. A method of creating different effects, textures, and *tone* variations in *printing* and *engraving* by using various special *screens*, or shading patterns.

Binding. The process of attaching loose pages together or attaching a cover to the pages, usually by gluing, saddle stitching (sewing wire through the center of the pages folded open), side stitching (stapling or otherwise binding *signatures* through the left edge), perfect binding (attaching signatures by adhesive along the book edge), and plastic and spiral binding (inserting spiral wire or plastic through slots punched into the left edge of pages).

Bleed. *Printing* that runs over the margins and off the edges of a sheet.

Block. See *Cut*.

Blowup. A photographic enlargement of a drawing, a photograph, or typography.

Blueprint. A final *proof* of material prepared for *offset printing*.

Blurb. A brief summary statement, such as a book-jacket blurb.

Boldface. A *typeface* that is heavy and dark, often used in headlines and other display type.

Bristol. Paper of various finishes and colors in postcard weight or heavier used for cards, announcements, posters, covers, and so on.

Broadside. A large sheet of paper, printed on one or both sides and folded to a smaller size, that reads as a single piece when opened.

Bullet. A solid ornamental dot, sometimes used to introduce items in a list.

Burnishing. Rubbing over something such as *Artype* to make it adhere to another surface.

Caps. Capital letters; also called *uppercase*.

Caption. The heading accompanying an illustration or other display. See also *Legend*.

Caret. A mark (∧) used in *copyediting* and proofreading to show where material is to be inserted.

Center spread. The two facing pages in the center of a publication.

Character count. The number of characters (letters, figures, spaces) in a line of typed *copy*.

Cold type. Type set by any means (for example, typewriter, word processor, photocompositor) other than by cast metal (*hot type*).

Column inch. A measure of space used by newspapers that is the equivalent of one inch deep and one column wide.

Combination plate. An *engraving* plate that has a *halftone* with either a *line drawing* or type.

Comp. Short for *comprehensive* and *compositor*.

Complementary colors. Any one of the *primary colors* yellow, red, and blue used in association with the remaining two primary colors combined (for example, yellow used with red and blue combined = yellow and violet).

Compositor. Also known as typesetter or comp; an operator who sets type.

Comprehensive. An elaborate, hand-prepared facsimile of

the proposed finished (printed) job, showing positions of type and illustrations; also called comp.

Continuous tone. An image such as a photograph that has gradations of *tone* from light to dark.

Copy. Manuscript material prepared for submission to a *compositor* or printer.

Copyediting. Correcting and improving written material in preparation for typing or typesetting.

Copyfitting. Estimating space and/or selecting type styles and sizes so that *copy* will fit into the available space on each page.

Copyright. The legal protection of and exclusive rights to literary, musical, or artistic property for a specified period.

Copywriting. Writing text and heads for an advertisement or a brochure.

Crop. To mark on an overlay or on the edges of a photograph the portions to be used in reproduction.

Cut. A zinc *etching* used in *letterpress printing;* any photo-*engraving;* loosely, any *halftone* (halftone cut) or *line drawing* (line cut).

Dead. A completed *printing* job ready for disposal or distribution.

Descender. The part of a *lowercase* (small) letter, such as *g, j, p, q,* and *y,* that extends below the *base line* of the letter.

Direct mail A method of advertising by mailing sales literatures such as letters, cards, and brochures directly to customers.

Display type. Heavy, large, or otherwise distinctive type.

Drop folio. A page number printed at the bottom of the page.

Dropout negative. A *halftone negative* with highlight dots exposed so that they do not appear on an *engraving* or *offset printing* plate.

Dry brush. The technique of preparing an art drawing by using a dry brush slightly moistened with India ink.

Dry mounting. Affixing photographs and other reproductions to backing boards by using a heated press and placing a tissue between the reproduction and its backing that melts under heat, binding the pieces together.

Dummy. A preliminary page-by-page *layout* of the job to be printed that labels and blocks off in exact size the space to be used for columns of type, headings, photographs, and so on. See also *Pasteup dummy*.

Duotone. A black-and-white photograph reproduced by making two plates, one for *printing* in a color and the other for printing in black, thereby creating color at a relatively low cost.

Editing. See *Copyediting*.

Em. The square of any size of type (one-em space in twelve-*point* type = twelve points square).

En. One-half of the square of any size of type (one-en space in twelve-*point* type = six points square).

End matter. See *Back matter*.

Endpapers. The paper pasted inside the front and back cover of a book connecting the cover to the inside pages.

Engraving. Short for photoengraving; a metal plate that has a relief *printing* surface made by photographing an image on the metal and then *etching*, or eating away the unwanted parts with acid.

Etching. Using acid to eat away the unwanted parts of an *engraving*, or metal plate; an impression made from an etched plate.

Fake process. A means of full-color reproduction in which an artist makes color separations by using overlays on the original *artwork* for each color desired. See also *Four-color process*.

Flat. A large sheet of paper, often yellow or orange, used in *offset printing*, with windows cut into it for taping *negatives* into position.

Flop. An instruction to the printer to turn a picture so that it faces the opposite way that it appears in a *proof*.

Flush. An instruction to a *compositor* or printer to set type or place *artwork* against the right or left margin.

Folder. A printed sheet folded to make separate pages.

Folio. Page number.

Font. An assortment of all characters in a particular size and style of type.

Format. The size, shape, style, and overall appearance of typed or printed material.

Four-color process. A color *halftone printing* process in which the *primary colors* and black are printed together to create a full range of colors.

Freelancer. A self-employed person such as a freelance writer who provides a service for others.

French fold. A sheet printed on one side and folded to make four pages.

Front matter. Preliminary pages such as the title page and the table of contents.

Frontispiece. An illustration positioned on a page facing the title page.

Full color. See *Four-color process*.

Full measure. Type set across a page or column to be flush with both the left and right margins.

Galley proof. A *proof* of type set in a galley (metal drawer or tray); generally, the first proof of material composed by any means.

Gang printing. Combining two or more *printing* jobs on one press run.

Gatefold. An oversize, foldout page, folded to fit the size of the publication.

Glossy. A photographic print made on shiny, coated paper for better tonal range in reproduction.

Gothic. See *sans serif*.

Grain. The direction in which fibers lie in paper, which determines the way the paper should be printed and folded.

Gravure printing. A method of *printing* using the intaglio process, in which images are etched into a plate and the depressions are filled with ink.

Gutter. The inside margins or space between the facing pages in a book.

Hairline. An extremely thin line; the finest rule that is used by printers.

Halftone. *Artwork* with *continuous tones*, such as a photograph, that can be broken up into a pattern of dots of different thickness from which a *printing* plate is made.

Halftone cut. See *Halftone*, *Cut*, and *Engraving*.

Hickey. A blemish.

Hot type. Type that is set by hand or machine using cast metal (for example, Linotype, Monotype, Intertype, and Ludlow), as opposed to *cold type*.

Imprint. *Printing* the name and address of a firm on previously printed material such as a catalog.

Indicia. Special permit notices authorized by the U.S.

Postal Service that are printed on envelopes or mailers instead of using postage stamps or metered tapes.

Initial letter. The first letter of text *copy* sometimes set in a size larger than the rest of the text.

Insert. Additional material, such as a reader-service card, that is usually printed separately and placed in the publication before *binding*.

Intaglio process. See *Gravure printing*.

Italic type. A *typeface* in which the characters have slanting lines.

Intertype. See *Hot type*.

Justify. To set type so that both the right and left sides of the lines of type are even, or of equal length.

Keying. Marking manuscript headings and other elements with numbers or letters that will help the *compositor* identify the elements (for example, A = first-level subhead, B = second-level subhead, and so on).

Kill. An instruction to the printer to delete certain material.

Layout. An artist's drawing, or blueprint, of a proposed piece that blocks off and identifies type and illustrations as they will appear in the final, printed version. See also *Comprehensive*.

Leading. Generally, the space between lines of type measured in *points;* inserting thin metal strips to separate lines of type in *hot-type* composition.

Legend. The written description of an illustration.

Letterpress printing. A method of *printing* from raised surfaces such as an *engraving*.

Lightface. A typeface lighter than the regular type.

Line cut. See *Cut*, *Engraving*, and *Line drawing*.

Line drawing. *Artwork* consisting of black lines on a white background with no tonal values such as you would find in a *halftone*.

Linotype. See *Hot type*.

Lithography. See *Offset printing*.

Logotype. A symbol used to identify an organization that appears on its stationery, products, and other material.

Lowercase (lc). Small letters such as *a*, *b*, and *c*.

Ludlow. See *Hot type*.

Machine composition. See *Hot type*.

Makeready. Preparing a press for *printing*.

Makeup. Preparing each page for reproduction by positioning typography and illustrations, often using a *dummy* or *pasteup dummy* as a guide, as they are to appear in the final printed version.

Mask. A protective cover placed over portions of *artwork* to avoid having them blemished with unwanted ink or paint.

Mat. Short for matrix; a paper mold, commonly used by newspapers in *letterpress printing*, from which a *stereotype* is made.

Matrix. See *Mat*.

Measure. The length of a line of type.

Mechanical. A finished piece of *artwork* (type, photos, art, and so on) ready for the camera; a camera-ready *pasteup*.

Monotype. See *Hot type*.

Montage. A group arrangement of type, *artwork*, and photographs that depicts something by way of a composite picture.

Multilith. A small *offset printing* press.

Negative. Photographic film made from *line drawings*, type, *halftones*, and other material and used to make a *positive* image on an *offset printing* plate.

Offset printing. A *printing* process in which an image is photographically transferred to a thin metal plate, and that image is "offset" to a rubber-blanketed cylinder that comes in contact with the paper to print on it.

Overlay. See *Acetate overlay*.

Overrun. The excess of printed copies over the number ordered.

Page proof. A *proof*, or copy, of typeset material that has been divided into pages.

Pasteup. A *mechanical*. See also *Pasteup dummy*.

Pasteup dummy. A *dummy* that shows the arrangement of material to be printed, with copies of the type, and sometimes of the illustrations, pasted on sheets of the same size as the proposed final product.

Perfect binding. See *Binding*.

Perforating. The process of cutting through a dashed or dotted line on printed material so that a portion of the material, such as a coupon, can easily be torn off by readers.

Photocomposition. See *Cold type*.

Photoengraving. See *Engraving*.

Photostat. A photographic copy of a *negative* or *positive* made directly on paper by a special camera; also called stat.

Pica. A basic unit of measure in *printing* (one pica = twelve *points* = ³/₁₆ inch).

Point. A measure of type size (1 point = ¹/₁₂ *pica* = ¹/₇₂ inch).

Positive. A photograph or *photostat* that corresponds to the original subject in terms of tonal values, as opposed to a *negative*, which reverses the values.

Primary colors. Yellow, red, and blue, the basic colors that are combined to create all other colors and, when used with black, to accomplish *four-color process* work.

Printing. The process of duplicating images on paper or some other surface as, for example, in *gravure printing*, *offset printing*, and *letterpress printing*.

Proof. A copy of material prepared for reproduction, such as a *galley proof*, *page proof*, *blueprint*, *silver print*, or *vandyke*, that is used to check for errors and defects.

Query. A question to the author or editor placed on a manuscript or *proof*.

Rate card. An information card (or sheet of paper) on which a magazine or newspaper lists its advertising rates and its requirements for preparing and placing ads.

Ream. A measure in the paper industry, usually five hundred sheets of any size. See also *Basis weight*.

Recto page. A right-hand page.

Relief. A *printing* process (for example, *letterpress*) that uses a raised surface, such as an *engraving*, that is inked to create an impression on paper.

Repro. Short for *reproduction proof*.

Reproduction proof. A final *proof*, with corrections made, pulled on coated paper ready for photographing to make *printing* plates.

Roman type. An ordinary typeface with straight letters, unlike an *italic* (slanted) face.

Rough. A *layout* without the precision or elaborate details of a *comprehensive*.

Saddle stitch. See *Binding*.

Sans serif. Modern, gothic *typefaces* without *serifs*, or strokes, along the tops and bottoms of letters.

Scaling. Computing the correct proportionate size (width and height) to which a photograph should be reduced to fit precisely in the space indicated on a *layout*.

Scoring. Creasing heavy paper for folding.

Screen. A cross-ruled sheet to break up a photograph into dots for reproduction; a *Benday* pattern used by engravers and *offset* printers to create a special effect; a transparent film with a pattern placed over a *mechanical* to create a special effect.

Secondary colors. Orange, green, and purple, colors created by mixing two of the *primary colors*.

Self-cover. A cover made of the same paper as the inside pages of a publication.

Self-mailer. A printed piece designed for mailing without an envelope.

Serif. A short line or stroke that crosses the ends (bottom and top) of a letter; the opposite of *sans serif*.

Side stitch. See *Binding*.

Signature. A large sheet of paper on which a number of pages (for example, eight, sixteen, thirty-two) are printed that fall into sequence after the sheet is folded and trimmed.

Silk screen printing. A stencil *printing* process that presses ink through a fabric screen to transfer the image onto another surface.

Silver print. A final *proof* of material prepared for *offset printing*.

Small caps (sc). Capital letters that are smaller than the regular *caps* in a piece of material.

Specifications. The technical details of a *printing* job, such as type size, column width, and *stock*.

Specs. Short for *specifications*.

Spine. See *Backbone*.

Stat. See *Photostat*.

Stereotype. A duplicate *printing* plate made from a paper *mat*.

Stet. An instruction to a *compositor* meaning "let it stand."

Stock. The paper on which *printing* is done.

Stripping. Placing *negatives* in *flats* to use in making *offset printing* plates.

Subscript. A small character that prints partly below the *base line*.

Substance. See *Basis weight*.

Superscript. A small character that prints partly above the *x-height*.

Tint. A color altered by the addition of white.

Tone. Color variation.

Trademark. A symbol, name, or device that identifies the origin of a product or the organization that makes it.

Transfer letters. See *Artype*.

Transparency. A color print placed on transparent film from which paper prints and *printing* plates can be made.

Trim size. The final size of printed material.

Typeface. A particular type design such as Spartan available in various sizes (for example, ten *point*) and weights (for example, **boldface**).

Typemark. Marking instructions to the *compositor* on a manuscript next to the various elements of *copy* (desired *typeface,* sizes, weights, *leading,* column widths, and so on) so that the typeset page will have the appearance and arrangement of copy that you want.

Typesetter. See *Compositor*.

Upper-lowercase (ulc). Capital and small letters as in *Writer's Almanac and Fact Book.*

Uppercase (uc). Capital letters such as *A, B,* and *C.*

Vandyke. A final *proof* of material prepared for *offset printing.*

Verso page. A left-hand page.

Wash drawings. An artist's drawing using lampblack paint diluted to various *tones* of gray to create the effect of a *halftone.*

Watermark. A manufacturer's design lightly pressed into the paper so that it can be seen when held up to the light.

White space. The blank area, or open space, around illustrations and typography in printed material.

Widow. An undesirable short line at the end of a paragraph that falls at the top of a page.

Word processor. A dedicated computer used in the preparation of written material; a software program used to direct the preparation of written material electronically. See also *Cold type.*

Wrong font (wf). A *typeface* set in error that is different from the others where it appears.

x-height. The height of the body of *lowercase* letters, without their *ascenders* and *descenders;* the height of the lowercase letter *x.*

INDEX

THE PRACTICAL
WRITER'S GUIDE

MARY A. De VRIES is the author of over
twenty business and professional books,
including *The Guide to Better Business
Writing, The Prentice-Hall Complete
Secretarial Letter Book,* and revised
editions of *The Complete Secretary's
Handbook.*